بسم الله الرحمن الرحيم

Imam Ibn al-Jawzi

Dhikr

Dhikr Publications.
First Published Sha'ban 1445AH
Febuary 2024.

Title: The Soul of Souls

Author: Abdul al-Rahman ibn al-Jawzi

Translation: Omer Siddique

ISBN Print: 978-0-6450379-6-8
ISBN Ebook: 978-0-6450379-7-5

Other Titles by Dhikr:
The Illumination on Abandoning Self-Direction.
Ibn Ata-illah Al-Sakandari

Sayidah A'isha: Wife to the Prophet, Mother
to a Nation. A Short Biography
Dr Muhammad Ramandan Al-Bouti

The Reviver of the Second Millenium:
Imam al-Rabbani Ahmed al-Sirhindi
Osman Nuri Topbas

dhikr.com.au

"Know that the life of this world is but play, idle talk, ornament, mutual boasting among yourselves, and vying for increase in wealth and children—the likeness of a rain whose vegetation pleases the farmers; then it withers such that you see it turn yellow; then it becomes chaff. And in the Hereafter there shall be severe punishment, forgiveness from Allah, and contentment, and the life of this world is naught but the enjoyment of delusion."

- Quran 57:20-21

Table of Contents

Imam Ibn al-Jawzi's Introduction

The slave, needy of his Nurturing Lord's forgiveness, Jamal ud-Deen, Abu al-Faraj, Abdul Rahman bin Ali bin al-Jawzi – may Allah be pleased with him and make Paradise his abode – says:

The praise belongs to Allah, Originator of all creatures, Prime Mover of the pen, Creator of existence out of nothingness. My praise falls short of the gratitude due to Him. I beseech Him for an increase of His bounty and benevolence and I send prayers upon His Messenger, Muhammad, His Prophet, and upon his Family, Companions, and his party.

The poet had spoken most eloquently and profoundly, and illustrated the choicest of methods, when he became aware of the truly great ones and so (comparing them to himself), his articulate tongue expressed, '*Adorning the eyes with antimony (kohl) is not the same as those naturally beautiful.*'[1] But if I was to remain silent, my preaching would remain unheard and, in the end, the command of Allah is pre-determined and decreed.

I request whoever reads this book of mine to generously offer excuses for any deficiencies that they find within.

Just as not every sound is pleasing and not every tree fruitful, may the reader take benefit from whatever of it might move their hearts and occupy their thoughts.

---

1 i.e., "I am only pretending to be like the pious and not really from amongst them."

I request, by the sanctity of Islam, that the reader supplicates to Allah that my end be upon Islam, that He forgives me when I return to Him, and my parents, and all Muslims.

I have organised this book into short sections and named it *Ruh al-Arwah* (*The Soul of Souls*). I ask Allah, that through it, the masses of Muslims benefit. Truly, He is All-Hearing, Answerer of Prayers.

Part One

The praise belongs to Allah, Alone in His Oneness, veiled from sight in this world by His Infiniteness. He is Alone in His Unity since before time. He is exalted above and beyond the words of deniers and their blasphemies. He fashioned the heavens into a spacious arena where stars, like horses, race from horizon to horizon as determined by the Pen of decree. He stretched out the Earth as a bed for creation so that His foregone planning and wisdom be manifested. He decreed death upon existence and so His command is executed without contention.

His order is accomplished throughout the heavens, upon the earth, throughout whatever is between them, and beneath the earth. He chained creation by acquainting them with duty and burden, testing them by what is heard and what is seen. He records their deeds so that each will read it, even those illiterate, on the Day of Taking into Account, '**the Day when every soul will find presented the good it did, and the evil it did...**'[2]

The praise belongs to Allah, Who alone has knowledge of what is concealed in chests and hidden in hearts. He has no partner in His creation, nor helper, nor collaborator, nor supporter. He is too Majestic to be constrained by a comparison, or by a form, or by a direction, or to any region. He is too sanctified to be encompassed by any thought, or to be restricted by any place, or to be perceived by any imagination. He is Exalted beyond being composed of substances or being confined by measure. Rather, He has composed the dust of creation,

2 Quran 3:30

mixing it with the inability of perceiving His Essence. Majestic is the One! The Overwhelming! The culmination of all existence is incomprehension of His Essence! How can it not be so, when man's nature is constrained by divine decree?

Man's purity is tarnished by lust and desire. His perception obscured by fixation with everything other than the Divine. Allah, Most Glorious, placed man between His order and prohibition, where man precariously sways between difficulties and peril. He enumerates their actions, small and great, on a register of deeds to be buried along with their bodies in a dark, deserted, and dilapidated home. There man lies, forgotten by companions. Visitors, fed-up with visiting him, trickle away and he wallows alone with his regrets. Such a long desolation! So far from one's (true and final) abode.

Then he shall be called to account for the deeds partaken by his hands. So, either towards gardens or fire he will proceed. '**On that Day the earth shall be changed into other than the earth, and the heavens (too), and they will appear before Allah, the One, the Paramount.**'[3]

Again, the praise belongs to Allah. Imaginings cannot reach Him nor do assumptions comprehend Him. He is cognisant of the occurring thought of the current moment and the deception hidden in eyes. He established Himself upon His Throne, and He is exalted above movement and stillness. He raised the heavens upon pillars of His Power, making it a settlement for angels, who never falter in praising Him. He has conducted them however

3 Quran 14:48

He willed, angels who '**do not disobey Allah in what He commands of them and who do what they are commanded.**'[4]

He has spread out the earth upon an overflowing sea. His irresistible command was given, and the sea was filled. He prepared the earth for creation and spread out their sustenance and so they find their nourishment therein. '**From it We created you, and unto it We shall bring you back, and from it We shall bring you forth another time.**'[5]

He sent messages to them, guiding them back to Him. As consequence, one person is accepted while another becomes embroiled in trial. Those who recognise reality roll up their sleeves, ready for hard work. While the heedless waste their time in amusements and desires. How long do the heedless sleep upon the mattress of idleness, never awaking? '**Till, when death comes unto one of you, Our messengers take him, and they neglect not their duty.**'[6]

Glorified be the One, who says to a thing, "Be!" And it is. I praise Him with the praise of one who knows that He knows what was, what is, what will be, and how what is not would be if it was! I bear witness that there is no god except Allah, Alone, with no partner – a testimony I entrust to Him on the day of my demise. I testify that Muhammad is His slave and messenger, the one to whom Allah entrusted profound knowledge and he

---

4 Quran 66:6
5 Quran 20:55
6 Quran 6:61

safeguarded it. May the prayers and blessings of Allah be upon him, his family, and his companions for as long as those who bow in prayer and those who prostrate do so.

To whom the vicissitudes of time speak, but he lends no ear. To whom warnings cry out, 'Return to the right path!' – yet he does not turn back. The doctor of preaching has taken your pulse and found your life afflicted with greed. Such inflammation there has been in your desires. How deep is the coma of your heedlessness.

You have outgrown the cloak of your youth. How long have you looked the other way? To what extent have you surrendered to your lusts? The dawn of grey hair is emerging, yet you build where you will not live and collect more than what you will need. If you were to lose a little wealth, you would be grieved. Yet, here you are, rejoicing in a life spent in amusements. Oh, if only that squandered time could return!

Have you not observed the lowering of loved ones into dirt? In a decrepit, neglected grave? From spacious homes they were relocated to horrors that no tongue can describe – '**the Day when every soul will find presented the good it did, and the evil it did...**'[7]

---

7 Quran 3:30

The Cobbler's Prayer

Muhammad ibn al-Munkadir narrates:
In the Masjid of the Messenger of Allah, may the peace and blessings of Allah be upon him, there was a pillar that I would sit by at night. One year, it did not rain on the people of Madinah, so they performed the prayer of seeking rain (*istisqa*) but to no avail. After praying the *isha* prayer one night at the Masjid, I went to lean on my pillar.

Soon, a light-skinned, African man appeared. He was wearing a yellow garment over himself and a shorter one over his shoulders. He came to the pillar that was directly in front of me, stood, performed the prayer, sat, and then said, '*O My Nurturing Lord...the people of Your Prophet, peace and blessings of Allah be upon him, went out praying for rain, yet You did not send down rain upon them. I beseech You to send rain upon them this very moment!*'

I said to myself that this man was certainly crazy! But he had not yet put down his hands when I heard thunder, and the heavens began to pour so much so that I worried about making my way back home. When he noticed the rain, he thanked Allah and praised Him with words I had never heard before. Then he said, '*Who am I and what am I that You answer me. Rather, You have been generous with allowing us to praise You and You have been generous with Your blessings.*'

He wrapped his shorter cloth over his head and threw down the other one between his feet. Then he stood for prayer and continued to pray until he sensed the approach of the *fajr* prayer. He prostrated, performed the *witr* prayer, prayed another two cycles of the *sunnah* of *fajr*, after which everyone joined together for the congregational f*ajr* prayer. When the prayer ended, the man left the Masjid, and I followed him. At the entrance gate, he lifted his garments and began wading through the water. I trailed behind him, lifting my robe as I ventured into the water, but lost sight of him.

The following night, I prayed at the Masjid as was my habit and retired to my pillar to lean on it. The man appeared again, wrapped his scarf over his head, threw his garment between his feet, prayed continuously until the *fajr* prayer, performed the *witr* prayer, prayed two cycles of the (*sunnah*) *fajr* prayer, then joined the congregational prayer, and I joined in with him. When the prayer was concluded, he got up to leave and I again followed him. He eventually entered a house that I recognised from my wanderings of Madinah. I returned to the masjid and when the sun had risen, I prayed before making my way back to that house. And there he was!

He was sitting, working as a cobbler. When he saw me, he knew who I was and said, '*Welcome Abu Abdullah! Are you in need of me making some shoes for you?*'
I sat by him and said, '*Are you not my companion from the other night?*'

His face changed and he shouted, '*O Ibn Munkadir how does that concern you!*' I sensed his anger and immediately got away. On the third night, I prayed *isha* at the Masjid of the Messenger of Allah, peace and blessings of Allah be upon him, retiring to my pillar afterwards. But this time he did not come. I thought to myself, 'What have

I done!' I stayed in the Masjid till the sun had risen and then left for that house. I arrived to find the door open and the house empty.

The owners of the house said to me, *'Abu Abdullah, what happened between you and this man yesterday?'*
I enquired, *'What happened to him?'*
They said, *'When you left him yesterday, he spread out his cloth in the middle of the house and then did not leave a thing – soft or hard – except he put it on his cloth. Then he made it a sack upon his back and left, and we do not know where he went!'*
There was not a single house in Madinah I knew of where I did not search for him, yet I could not find him.

Seeking out the Lovers of Allah

I roam in search of my Beloved, unbeknownst to many,
If people felt the sting of passion, they too would crave.

Is the lover's life not marked by woeful torment?
Filled with cries and ceaseless yearning?

My heart aches when a scent wafts from afar,
Where in the verdant gardens the dove coos.

Night left, yet the darkness lingered,
Like a seal imprinted by that distant scent.

How many exist without love's touch, in slumber?
While the lover's eyes remain ever wakeful.

Destiny commanded that the lovers forsake sleep,
As if the dreams of lovers are forbidden.

Longing has consumed their bodies and hearts,
Leaving naught but a skeletal frame.

I wandered into their gatherings and echoed their names,
Overwhelmed by deep sighs and fervour.

In lush gardens stand their tents,
To which I, for as long as I breathe, send my greetings.

You, whose hopes stretch far for what is short-lived! What a wretched slave you are! It is as if the Lord says, *Have I not nourished you with My Kindness? Did I not create you Myself? Did I not breathe into you of My spirit?*[8] *Have you not realised how I deal with those who defy Me? Are you not ashamed when you remember Me in your trials and forget Me in your comfort? The clarity of your intuition (baseerah) has been blinded by your lusts – so how will you recognise Me? This is an exhaustive admonition, why then are you so indifferent? If you reconcile with Me through righteousness, upon you I bestow your wishes. Set aside this world, the best of which is tainted and the hopes of which are wishful thinking. Woe unto you! You have traded closeness with Me for what is insignificant, when to Me there is no second. What shall be your response when your limbs shall bear witness against you, recounting what you saw and heard? On* ***'the Day when every soul will find presented the good it did, and the evil it did...'***[9]

8 See Quran 15:29
9 Quran 3:30

Sa'doun the Madman

Yahya ibn Ayoub narrates:

One day I went out to the cemetery at *Bab al-Khurasan.* I sat at a place where I could see whoever enters the graveyard. A man with his face veiled eventually entered. He began wandering around the graves and every time he saw an old grave that was opened to accept a new occupant (the previous corpse being completely decomposed), he stood over it, weeping.

I stood up to make my way towards him, hoping to benefit from him. I reached him and alas! It was *Sa'doun,* who the people would call a madman. He would live in a shack in the cemetery situated on the burial plot of *Abdullah ibn Malik.*

I called out to him, *'O Sa'doun! What are you doing here?'* He replied, *'O Yahya, shall we sit and weep over these bodies that have decomposed into dust?'* Then he said after a moment, *'O Yahya! It is more proper, by Allah, that we weep out of regret (over our sins and wasted days) than we weep over these decomposed bodies! O Yahya, "**and when the pages are spread...**"*[10].*'* Then he cried out at the top of his lungs, *'Save me! O Allah! O Allah! Save me from the pages spread!'*

On hearing this, I lost consciousness. When I came to, he was sitting by me, wiping my face with his sleeve. He said, *'O Yahya! Who would be more honoured than you if you*

10 Quran 81:10. When the pages are spread refers to the opening of the record of peoples' deeds on the Day of Judgement. Upon seeing their entire life's deeds, they will say, "'**What a book this is! It leaves out nothing, small or great, save that it has taken account thereof.' And they find present [therein] whatsoever they did.**" (Quran 18:49). On that day, every deed will need to be answered for, save what Allah wills.

had died in your very place!'[11]

Forsake Me Not My Lord

You have laden me with Your love, too much to bear,
You've intoxicated me so, that I find no way to sobriety.

Yet You have barricaded me, a locked door before You,
Since it is You, we have no key to pry it open.

You've set me aflame, aggravating my yearning,
With passing moments, my craving for You intensifies.

My sighs are a witness to the blaze within,
Inside me, love smoulders, a relentless fire.

If tears of separation are not shed for You,
For what else could they possibly be shed for?

When will I find relief in closeness with You?
On any day, there is no one else comparable.

No comfort for the ardent lovers, filled with longing,
Neither in separation nor in proximity does comfort dwell.

Mercy, O Lord, for this ailment You've inflicted me with,
For the healer is forever a companion of the ailing patient!

You, who keep tripping over the robe of your lusts! When will the dawn of repentance appear? You, whom the darkness of youth has deceived, the rays of white hair have already arisen. Have you exhausted your strength in seeking the worldly, but in old age hope for piety? O seasoned veteran of idleness! The advance of years has clipped one of the wings of your firm resolve. Your hopes

11 i.e., What an honourable ending of your life it would have been, with which you could meet Allah.

reach to distant lands, but your funeral is close enough to occur tomorrow morning.

Where are those who fortified mansions, certain of tomorrow's amusements and comforts? Time has obliterated them; how many screams are there now within grand tombs – if only you could hear. One of them dreams of an hour of your life for reprieve and to rest in peace from the torment of the grave.

O congregation of sinners! Such is the funeral ceremony of the miserable ones. Where is the weeping? Where are the wails of sorrow? If my warnings leave you unaffected like a physician does a dying man, then your illness has indeed intensified. Sharpen the sword of your faith and renounce your inclination to this world. Perhaps you will catch up with those of sound health. The squanderers of their lives will regret when the veils are lifted, '**On the Day the earth shall be changed into other than the earth, and the heavens [too], and they will appear before Allah, the One, the Overpowering.**'[12]

The Illustrious Pauper

Jafar Al-Saqaa narrates:

One rainy day, I went out and came across a sick, African man lying besides a heap of rubbish. I dragged him into my house and later in the evening, he called out to me saying, '*O Abu Jafar! Do not thwart my plan!* (To meet Allah in a humble state). *Sit down next to me.'* All the while, a pleasant smell of musk was filling the house until even my robe, garments, utensils, even my grandmother,

12 Quran 14:48

everything in the house smelled if it.

'*Sit next to me,*' he said and at the same time gestured with his hands that I do not get too close as if to spare room for others. '*Come down closer my brothers,*' he continued to say. '*Be gentle with me, O Allah, O my Refuge!*' Then he gave up his soul.

I began thinking to myself that I will sell my garment so that I could buy a shroud for him for his burial. Suddenly the door was knocked, and people came one after the other saying, '*Has someone with you died that requires a shroud, O Abu Jafar?*'

I complain to You of my agony and yearning,
And when I meet You with overflowing eyes.

And of burning settled in my heart,
What no healer can hope to heal.

What of Our past rapport, what calamity has fallen?
Oh my broken bonds, vows, and sacred covenants!

Have you so taken my heart, leaving but a lifeless form?
A husk remains, for whom have You preserved it?

You have flung me aside, abandoned in a quagmire,
Tears are my refreshment, with Your memory, I drink.

Whom do I commission to send You my greetings?
Who can relay of my distress and my yearning?

O Beloved, beyond need for this petty lover
Is there a chance You send a glance this way?

What is this state of yours? How often has your heart been counselled, yet you remain deaf to its wisdom? You have lost your youth in heedlessness and weep in your old age? How readily have you found comfort in the bed of sin? Who is more blind than you? You disobey the One who created you from a sperm-drop, Who has complete power over you and the power of decree over you.

In His grasp are the treasuries of the heavens and the earth. He asks of you a goodly loan, and He takes from you as He wills, and whatever you have is insignificant. He owns the seas overflowing and asks from you just a tear drop to put out the inferno of Hell. Have your eyes had enough of reverence and fear? Will you not draw wisdom from those who passed before you? Does wretchedness stem from anything but a soul unwilling to change? But is there any doctor for the deaf? Or medicine for the blind?

My Brethren, through Allah's help strive towards repentance before all your secrets are unveiled, '**On the Day the earth shall be changed into other than the earth, and the heavens [too], and they will appear before Allah, the One, the Overpowering.**'[13]

The Reverent Neighbour

Abu Hisham relates:
A woman from the people of Yemen came to us. Her name was *Shabunah,* and she settled in our district. At nights, I would hear weeping and whimpering from her home. I said to my maid, '*Go out and look at this woman*

13 Quran 14:48

to see what she is doing.' She did so and found her to be standing facing the *qibla,*[14] raising her face to the heavens. I asked, *'What was she doing?'*

'I did not see her doing anything other than keeping her eyes fixed at the sky,' she replied.

'Listen to what she says,' I said.

The maid replied, *'I do not understand most of her words, but I did catch her saying:*

I see that You have arranged her (referring to herself) from clay. You covered her with Your blessings. You nourish her from spiritual state to spiritual state, and every state You made for her, You made it as a paradise. She sees as good all Your trials upon her. But she is still liable to Your wrath by continuing in Your disobedience. Does she think that You do not see her bad deeds? But You Witness all things!

She said that, let out a shriek, and fell to the ground.'

The maid had informed me of her fainting and when morning came, we went to investigate, but she had died.

The Eyes of the Lovers of God Never Sleep

I roam in my longing, a quest for the Beloved
When I catch hold of a bolt of lightning glistening.

I find myself seeking Him, stomach churning
When I feel from Him a breeze caressing.

Love for Him grows in every heart, a cure
For the crestfallen, but a balm more potent.

His memory ensnares the grief-stricken
Seizing hearts, returning with captives in tow.

---

14 Direction of prayer, to Mecca.

And how every heart drips adoration for His Name
With an aroma like honey, but in flavour richer.

For when the remembrance of the Beloved takes flow
Soft hearts are broken and stern ribs, crushed.

He has a throne in many a heart, as if
He graces each, a garden of paradise, eternal.

His qualities outshine the metaphors of lovers
But let the hopeful praise Him still filled with yearning.

Woe to you! How much have you competed in sin against the One Who bestows on You power and ability? O wayward slave, how far off the path of the One Who fashioned you have you strayed? Do you think He has forgotten your deeds? Rather He only delays your punishment. If you walk to good deeds, it is with slackness, but towards sin, how you rush!

O captured one in the prison of heedlessness, thinking you are free! Your desires and lusts have blinded your true intuition (*baseerah*), you are in a disastrous predicament. You have filled your record of deeds with sins while the Angel of Death prepares his visit. The river of your life is about to spill over, old age is near, and your strength is diminishing.

Woe to you, is it not yet time for you to hasten, with every fibre of your being, towards the shores of repentance? Is it not time for your ears to yield and accept guidance?

Oh, if only I knew what else occupies your mind. Let not this chapter end without beginning your determination to repent. Be not expelled from His mercy. When you see the banners of the remorseful passing by, join your hopes to theirs. Rush to make amends at the door of the Beloved before the decree of the King unexpectedly descends. Do so before you regret – when regret and excuses will hold no benefit – '**On the Day the earth shall be changed into other than the earth, and the heavens [too], and they will appear before Allah, the One, the Overpowering.**'[15]

A Bridge Like This

Ibn Subh relates:
I said to *Abdullah al-Barrani, 'Why your continual weeping, day and night?'*

He stretched out his hand to me and on his finger there was a single intertwined hair. He straightened it out and said, *'O Saeed, if we are to pass over a bridge like this (the* sirat[16]*), which foot will be able to keep its footing?'* He then began to weep.

Allah, Only You are Our Hope!

When will a gift from You grace our wretchedness,
Be not harsh with us nor annoyed.

Alas! You made us ill with Your long absence
By the sanctity of love, return and visit us.

By the solemn vows of Your intimate covenant,
If it pleases You to test us so, then let the trials ascend!

---

15 Quran 14:48

16 It has been related that the Prophet (s) said, "Above Hellfire there is a bridge, thinner than a hair and sharper than a sword..." – Shu'ab Al-Iman, Imam Bayhaqi

Torment us to Your heart's content, O Beloved!
Just cast us not away from the mat before Your door.

What humiliation for one who craves after other than You
Or aches for closeness to other than You, what a madman!

Revive us with the warmth of Your proximity
With a welcome, greet us and give us life!

Woe to you! When you participate in gatherings you make the false promise of 'I repent!' You who seek the temporary while the Eternal seeks you. O *Yousef* of sorrow, when will you reunite with *Yacoub*? You who claim to seek worldly things only out of necessity, while annihilation seeks you. How much of your life's preciousness has been robbed by the passing days, leaving you plundered?

O one shackled by this world's deception, you are a prisoner to its guards of worldly desires. Do you not know that every breath of yours is written? You walk upright but your heart, in its deviance, is dragged on its face! A body alive but a heart dead. Outwardly victorious, but inwardly humiliated. For how much longer will your Guardian call you, but you will not repent? If the caravan of the hard-striving ones happens to pass you by, follow them, be it even in the late hours of night prayer. Perhaps you will receive a kindness from the Beloved. But those excluded from the door of the Beloved, they are far astray. **"Until, when death comes to one of them, he says, 'My Lord, send me back!'"**[17]

---

17 Quran 23:99

The Secret Deed

Dhu'l Nun al-Misri narrates:

The people went out to perform the prayer for rain (*istisqa'*) in Basra and I went out with them. While I was amongst the people, suddenly two hands grabbed my legs. I said, *'Who are you? Let me be!'*

He replied, *'I am Sa'doun the Madman. Where are you headed, O Abu al-Fayd?'*

'To the place of prayer, to beseech Allah, Glorious and Exalted,' I answered.

'Is it with a heavenly heart or a heart empty?' He asked.

'With a heavenly heart,' I responded.

Then he said, *'Look here Dhu'l Nun! Do not adorn and embellish yourself with pride for the One to call to account is All-Seeing. Shall you pray and I say ameen to your prayer, or shall I pray, and you say ameen to my prayer?'*

'You pray and I will say ameen,' I answered.

He stood up and said, *'O My Lord! I beseech You by what happened yesterday, that You send down rain this very moment!'*

By Allah, I saw clouds gathering from my right and my left and joining together, they began pouring rain like buckets. I said to him, *'I ask you by the One you Worship, what happened between you and Allah yesterday?'*

'Do not come between me and the apple of my eye!' He retorted.

'You must inform me,' I pleaded.

Instead, he began chanting the following lines:

I was amicable with Him and don't desire any other
For fear of slipping and losing sight of His splendour.

Enough it is, a regret, a sickness, and weakness
To be even driven out from the gatherings of His friends.

Then he left me, turning away in escape. May Allah be pleased with him.

Do not Enter Between the Beloved & I

The lover's claim is empty if he does not dissolve
On the day of parting, then it is a lie told!

It is separation! Spend what you have gathered for this day
In the vault of tears and gather what was squandered of sorrow.

Be generous with your devotion, though no reward in sight
The stingiest of people, is the lover of little sorrow.

Say to your heart – 'Ignore those who blame you!'
For the noblest heart, beats not for another.

Don the decorated cloak of love and deep desire
And yearning like vapour, and tears like downpour.

Our Beloved, after You distanced from Your lovers
Their lives turned to beggary and abject poverty.

You went far, so did we, and unbridled tears
Like horses, galloped from eyes down to our sides.

When the cool breeze breathes life to me anew
I yearn for You from the intensity of ecstasy.

When I remember the days of our shared adoration
The shaking of my heart compounds its desperation.

Where are those golden nights, standing captive in Your charm
As if they were spun of nothing but pure, gold yarn.

If You wish to pluck any fruit from my humble tree
Take what You will, no resentment, nor fatigue you'll find from me!

You, who have grown tired of worship, and with empty hopes for repentance! If only I knew on what you have spent the fruits of your youth! In your season of bloom and freshness, you kept yourself absent from the beloved ones, the righteous. Yet now, as you wither and dry, you seek the threshold of their doors.

How many companions have you concealed beneath the earth? Have you not seen how their close friends and peers now shun and avoid them? As if neither they nor we had ever been together in friendship or community. They were relocated to the home of grief, where no prayer for return is ever answered. How incredible that all these gatherings of remembrance have not altered you. Your body is present in the gathering, but your heart is elsewhere, so who will listen to this address?

If your heart is not moved by my exhortation, then know, that everything that is yours above the earth but waits until you are beneath it. You will witness firsthand the disgrace and humiliation that befall the rebellious. '**Until, when death comes to one of them, he says, "My Lord, send me back!"**'[18]

Even if You Forgive, You Still Know the Sin

It has been related that *Fudayl ibn Ayyad* stood on the day of *Arafah* (during the *Hajj*). While the people were asking Allah, he was weeping like a mother mourning her child. When the sun was about to set, he clutched his beard, and raising his head to the heavens, he said, "*Oh what*

18 Quran 23:99

fathomless disgrace (my sins bring) before You – even if You forgave them..."

Return my Sanity O Lord

O gentle, persistent breeze, will you not grant us solace?
Perhaps we may mend from the pain of love's remembrance.

Be my messenger, bearing regards returned
To my Beloved, deliver a thousand greetings!

The returning dove did not ignite my longing
Rather my passion taught longing to the dove.

A wonder is the loss of my heart after You
How have I, devoid of it, endured?

My mind too is with you, return please a portion
So I may thank You for this love's anguish and longing.

These reminders are as if a garden, adorned with roses. Its knowledge more fragrant than cologne, its branches leaning down, laden with fruits. Its meanings, freshly plucked, are within arm's reach so any mind can grasp them. Its river stretches far, as if drawing wisdom from the ocean's depths.

The birds of its eloquence sing upon branches of fine expression. Their songs fill those well-versed in understanding with delight. How many pearls of wisdom are scattered around its edges. How many paths of the esteemed are paved within. Its precious stones have been handpicked, as if fallen from the seal-rings of the intimately righteous (*arifeen*). Its magnificent jewels of spiritual states have been gathered to aid the seekers. But its most matchless, precious pearls are accessible only to the spiritual elite. Yet it is still aplenty with clear parables of subtle meaning that are antimony even on the eyes of the simple-minded, even if their meanings be deep and elevated.

My Lord! What am I to do? What course could I embark upon? I have not yearned for the Hereafter as it should be yearned for. My longing for this fleeting world has turned out to be in error. It has scarred procrastination into my very essence. It has made me sit on the sidelines of righteous action. And now the debt of old age is due and demands immediate payment. In the court of judgement, my poverty of good deeds is proven. Hence, confine me in the prison of proper patience and have mercy on my desolation. I have no saviour other than You. No worthy deeds to be counted as offspring, no knowledge that could be considered an ancestor. There is just the filled treasury of Your mercy, only the vast charity of Your forgiveness. If You overlook sins it is due to Your grace and if You punish, it is by Your justice – and in both cases the praise and gratitude is Yours!

My Brethren, whoever has a condition similar to mine, I appeal to you by Allah, once memory of me has faded, remember me in your prayers — that Allah have mercy upon my desolation and that He remembers me with His mercy.

Part Two

All praise belongs to Allah, who made Himself known to His friends (*awliya*) with the profound gravity of His Grandeur and they recognised Him. With affection and love He accustomed them to withstand their awe of Him. He bestowed on them depths of knowledge, and they recognised that it is only through His remembrance of them that they are able to remember Him. His angels boast of the spiritual states of His friends and how could they not, when He has loved His friends, and they love Him. He sheltered the sanctuaries of their hearts from the knockings of heedlessness of Him. They preserved the harvest of their good deeds in the vault of pure sincerity – and then they sealed it. They scrutinised notebooks of their deeds, making amends for any lapses. They fear being embroiled in scandal on the Day of Reckoning, so they safeguarded Allah's trust upon them. They attained what the Beloved promised them and received more than what they asked for. As for the deprived, they are in the wasteland of rejection, having been outcast and refused mercy. What humiliation they will face at the Gathering, donning shirts of disgrace – '**on the Day when faces whiten and faces blacken…**'[19]

Praise belongs to Allah, the Originator of all existing things, He is without partner or helper. Exalted be He in His greatness, transcendent from having characteristics of originated and classified things. He established Himself over the Throne and His mercy descends to accept the repentance of the penitent. '**The whole earth shall be but a handful to Him on the Day of Resurrection, and**

---

19 Quran 3:106

the heavens will be enfolded in His grasp.'[20] What an excellent grasp it is!
'Who made beautiful all that He created, and Who began the creation of man from clay.'[21]

He created man from a vile drop and carried him through the stages of existence – but alas, man becomes an outright adversary! He empowered desires to reign over them, so they recognise their degradation and humility. But the eyes of sinners are dry of weeping, so they find no helper. The devotees of Allah stand at His door, enticed by their Beloved, Who lovingly beckons, '**And hasten unto forgiveness from your Nurturing Lord, and for a garden whose breadth is the heavens and the earth.'**[22]

Praise belongs to Allah, Who is not changed by events nor worn away by the procession of time. He is the First, but He has no second. He is the Last, but not bounded by the cessation of time. He is the Apparent, known through observation of His creation. He is the Hidden, so what He is cannot be defined. '**He knows the treachery of eyes and that which breasts conceal.'**[23] He is not body, nor substance, nor is He subject to chance or contingency, nor is He the elements, nor is He nature. The one who denies His Attributes is eyeless, the one who denies His existence is blind, the one who attributes a body to Him is dim-sighted, and the one likening Him to His creation is ensnared in the prison of negligence and ignorance.

He causes water to shower from the heavens, resurrecting

20 Quran 36:67
21 Quran 32:7
22 Quran 3:133
23 Quran 40:19

fruits, some on trees, others on soil. He transforms water into nourishment and into living creatures, both female and male. He manifests His bounty and His justice – elevating some, breaking others. He engraved on the tablets of their souls, on the day of their creation, the letters of delight and those of sorrow.

Thus, each soul journeys towards the unknown, for He hid the ultimate outcomes from them. He shoots the arrows of death at them, hitting the mark, striking their throats. Then, so that they know He is Just and does not oppress, He consoled them, '**Every soul shall taste death, and you will indeed be paid your rewards in full on the Day of Resurrection. And whosoever is distanced from the Fire and made to enter the Garden has certainly triumphed. And the life of this world is naught but the enjoyment of delusion.**'[24]

Exalted above every imperfection is He, Who Decrees but is not decreed upon. He shatters what is whole, He mends what is broken. I praise Him with the recognition of one hopeful of His mercy, knowing full well that He is the Especially Merciful, the Oft-Forgiving. I bear witness that there is no god except Allah, He alone, and no partner has He – a testimony that I prepare for the Day of Unfoldings. I bear witness that Muhammad is His slave and messenger, intercessor of the nation on the day when those in their graves are resuscitated. The blessings of Allah be upon him, his family, and his companions as long as the ages and time endure.

My Brethren, whoever of you exhausts himself to attain

---

24 Quran 3:185

what he is leaving behind, have you not witnessed the cameleer of night and day guiding away your departing life? Have you not seen night and day take off with lives never returned? Have you not glimpsed at the one who napped beneath this life's shade, how well can the short-lived one be shaded? Have you not heard of the one who lived a thousand years and then said, 'I remained only a few days'? What of those that erected grand castles and formidable fortresses? They were vanquished by the sword of death, each one lost his kingdom.

Where are the peoples of *Nuh, 'Ad* and *Thamud*? Where are the people of *Tubba*? Where are the bygone kings? Where are those whose realms reached to the East and to the West? They departed, reaping no benefit. They were carried to a shadowy home where there is no difference between sultan and simpleton. Their landmarks were effaced, returning back to dust, obliterated as a basic lesson for both the knowledgeable and the ignorant. Will you not now hear their silent shouts? Will you not awaken, O heedless one? Where are the thrones? Where is *al-Nu'man*?[25] Where is Khosrow? Where are their pavilions? What of Babel's kings? All were swept away by the relentless march of nights and days, adjourned till a day in which they will bring forth all that they prepared. '**On the Day when faces whiten and faces blacken...**'[26]

---

25 Possibly al-Numan ibn al-Mundhir, a pre-Islamic, Arabian ruler.

26 Quran 3:106

A Rose in the Desert

Abdul Wahid ibn Zayd narrates:

For three nights, I beseeched Allah to show me my destined wife in Paradise. I dreamt of a voice saying to me, *'O Abdul Wahid, your wife in Paradise is Maymouna al-Sawdah! '*

'Where is she?' I queried.

'In the tribe of so and so, in Kufa.'

So, I set out to Kufa and inquired about her. I was told, *'She is a mad woman amongst us and tends to a few of our goats!'*

'I wish to see her, 'I insisted.

They finally directed me, *'Then venture towards the desert.'*

So, I set off and found her standing in prayer. Her staff was placed in front of her, and she was wearing a woollen cloak, upon which it was written 'Not bought and not sold.'[27] Remarkably, her goats were alongside a pack of wolves, neither did the wolves attack the goats, nor did the goats flee from the wolves.

When she noticed me approaching, she shortened her prayer and said, *'Go back Ibn Zayd! Here is not our meeting place. That shall be another day.'*

'May Allah extend His mercy upon you! Who has informed you that I am Ibn Zayd?' I asked.

She answered, *"Do you not know that souls are mobilised soldiers, whoever they were mutually acquainted with (in*

27 This could mean that she will not be enticed by this world (be bought) or allow herself to submit to anyone (be sold) as she sees herself bought and owned only by Allah. Or it could mean that she sees herself so insignificant that she is something none would bother to buy or sell. And Allah knows best.

the realm of souls), they have affinity with, and whoever they rejected, they differ with'[28]*?"*

I said to her, *'Advise me.'*

She replied, *'How peculiar that a preacher be preached to. O Ibn Zayd! Stamp righteous expressions upon your limbs (i.e., perform righteous actions with them), and you will learn what escapes others. O Ibn Zayd! It has reached me that if a slave of Allah is granted something of this world, yet desires more (i.e., is not content), Allah, Glorified and Majestic, strips him of the sweetness of being in solitude with Him. He exchanges the closeness between them for distance and friendliness for desolation.'* Then she began to recite:

You seek to heal others, yet illness in you resides,
A shy fault within your own soul that hides.

O Preacher, for Allah's name, take your stand,
Guiding others from sin with an honest hand.

Had you but corrected your faults of old,
Repentance might have embraced you in its fold.

And then, my dear, with a voice, sweet as the birds'
Hearts, young and old, would be wombs for your words.

But alas, you preach against sin with fervour,
And indulge in it yourself, without a quiver!

I said to her, *'I see wolves alongside sheep with neither the sheep being alarmed by the wolves nor the wolves attacking the sheep. How is this happening?'*

She replied, *'Leave me be. I restored my relationship with my Master and so, He restored the relationship between the wolves and the sheep.'* The she began to recite:

28 Hadith. Riyad as-Salihin 371

Let Nothing Come Between My Love for Allah

If you saw me on the day of union, entranced with another
You would not find me seeing sweetness in desert's water.

If not for pining's caress, love's taste I'd never know,
Never would I unveil the secrets my heart does stow!

Oh, my heart! With each day of separation and exile,
You forge in me the arts of love, its mastery, and style.

The Beloved's absence tears within, a scream of grief confined,
And modesty's gentle hold keeps the agony enshrined.

I ache for You, held captive in separation's bitter clasp,
How I yearn to be near You, in Your presence, bask.

Fever gave way to anguish, longing profound
Madness it seems, this passion I've found.

Sleep shunned my eyes, left them wide with dismay,
I thought they'd forgotten how to close, lost their way.

To find another like You, an impossibility so true,
Impossible that my heart betray its love for You.

O distracted one in his youth, will not the dawn of white hair awaken the rising of repentance? When the branches of your youth were tender and supple, you freely swayed to sin and postponed seeking forgiveness. Time and again you were invited but how often have you turned a deaf ear? Varieties of wrongs weigh you down, preventing you from ascending towards the Beloved. You neither join the caravan of those that strive, nor do you partake in the offerings of the forgiveness-seekers. The hospital that is your heart can be full of well-wishing visitors, but you seek no doctor to diagnose your sickness that they may appear. Your home of the hereafter is in tatters, but this temporary house is well furnished?

Seeing your state, your anxious and depressed intelligence asks, 'Many men have reached the gardens of Eden, yet here you remain, robbed bare, the journey barely begun?' Look at the riches of this world awaiting you – a crown of fake-silver strands of hair and a matching white shroud.

But what use, if your body stands before me and your heart is ensnared in another realm's dark pit? To whom shall I address? For whom do I gather these words? How can I sweeten such bitterness, even with all the waters of the Tigris? You do not ascend to the heavenly heights of those that strive with great effort. Neither do you cross the bridge of examining your deeds, nor do you learn to swim across. How will you then reach the shore of the Beloved?

O companion of the forgiveness-seekers, hurry! The descent into the grave approaches soon. Hoard your rations! You shall find your provisions of God-mindfulness (*taqwa*) stored for you '**on the Day when faces whiten and faces blacken…**'[29]

The Fellowship of the Faithful

Salih al-Marri narrates:
One day, *Malik ibn Dinar* said to me, '*Let us head out to meet Salih al-Jabban. I promised him and a group of my brothers that we would visit the blind shaykh, Abu Juhayn Masood, today.*'

29 Quran 3:106

We set out to meet *Salih al-Jabban* and I was pleased to find the brothers had gathered and amongst them were *Muhammad bin Wasie'*, *Thabit al-Banani*, and *Habib al-Ajmi*. I thought to myself, 'By Allah, this is truly a blessed day!' And so, we set out for *Abu Juhayn*.

It was the custom of *Malik ibn Dinar* to say to *Thabit* whenever coming across a clean piece of land, '*O Thabit, pray here. Perhaps it will bear witness*[30] *for you on a coming day.*' We left *Thabit* to pray awhile and carried on.

When we reached the house of *Abu Juhayn*, we asked about him. We were told, '*He will come out soon to go for the prayer,*' so we waited. Eventually, a man came out leading *Abu Juhayn* by the hand to the masjid (since he was blind), leaving him standing near its gate. *Abu Juhayn* appeared emaciated, as if he had just come out of his grave. He prayed however much Allah willed, then the call for the congregational prayer was given and we all prayed behind him as the imam.

When the prayer had finished and he was sitting in a grief-stricken state, people crowded around him to offer their greetings. The first amongst us to go forward was *Muhammad bin Wasie'* who gave his greetings. *Abu Juhayn* responded and then said, '*Allah have mercy upon you. Who*

---

30 Abu Hurairah (rad) reported: The Messenger of Allah, peace and blessings of Allah be upon him, recited the verse, '**That Day it (the earth) shall convey its news.**' (99:4) Then he asked, 'Do any of you know what its news is?' They replied, 'Allah and His Messenger know best.' He said, 'Truly, its news is that it bears witness what every male-slave and female-slave did on its back. It will testify: You did such and such on this or that day. This is its news.' Riyad as-Salihin 408.

am I speaking to?'

'Just a man from the people of Basra,' he replied.

'What is your name?' Abu Juhayn insisted.

'Muhammad bin Wasie'.'

Abu Juhayn replied, *'Welcome! The people of this town say you are the best of them in the sight of Allah. Let yourself be thankful to Him. Sit down here.'* So, he sat near him.

Next, *Thabit al-Banani* went forward and greeted him. He returned the greeting and asked, *'Allah have mercy upon you. Who am I speaking to?'*

'Thabit al-Banani,' he replied.

'Welcome! The people of this town claim you are the longest of them in performing prayer. Sit down here, I was wishing to meet you!'

Then it was the turn of *Habib al-Ajmi*, who offered his greetings. *Abu Juhayn* returned his greeting and asked, *'Allah have mercy upon you. Who am I speaking to?'*

He replied, *'Habib.'*

'Welcome! The people of this town claim that you do not ask anything from Allah, Mighty and Glorious, except that He grants it to you. You should ask Him to hide this for you from the people. Sit here, Allah's mercy be upon you!' And *Abu Juhayn* took him by the hand and seated him right by his side.

Malik ibn Dinar then went forth and greeted him. He returned the greeting and asked, *'Allah have mercy upon you. Who am I speaking to?'*

'Malik ibn Dinar,' he replied.

'Bravo! Bravo! The people of this town claim you are the most abstinent of them to this world. Sit here. Now, my wish from my Nurturing Lord, Mighty and Glorious, has been fulfilled!'

Finally, I (*Salih al-Marri*) pounced forward and greeted

him. He returned my greeting and asked, *'Allah have mercy upon you. Who am I speaking to?'*
I replied, *'Salih al-Marri.'*
'You are the young reciter of the Qur'an?' He questioned.
'Yes,' I replied.
'Read, O Salih.'

I began to read and had barely begun when *Abu Juhayn* suddenly lost consciousness. He was revived but said again, *'Return to your recitation, O Salih.'*

I returned to my reading and when I reached '**And We shall turn to whatever work they have done and make it scattered dust. That Day the inhabitants of the Garden shall have the best dwelling place and the most beautiful rest**'[31] – he let out a shriek and fell forward, part of his body becoming uncovered. He began to bellow like a bull before falling silent. We came close to him and alas, his soul had departed, may Allah have mercy upon him. We went out and asked, *'Does he have a family?'* We were told that there is an old woman who comes to serve him from time to time. We sent for her, and she asked, *'What happened to him?'*
We answered, *'The Qur'an was recited to him, and he passed away.'*
She said, *'By Allah, he (Abu Juhayn) spoke the truth. Who is the one who recited to him, is it perhaps Salih the Qur'an reciter?'*
'Yes, ' we replied, *'and how do you know Salih?'*
'I do not know him, but how often I would hear Abu Juhayn say that if Salih were to recite the Qur'an to me, he would kill me.'
'He is the one who recited the Qur'an to him!'

31 Quran 25:23-24

'He is the one that has killed my beloved one,' she replied. We then shrouded him and buried him. May the mercy of Allah be upon him.

O dwellers of the city of sin, when will you abandon the house of heedlessness? Time's relentless march will bring down your citadels, built since the days of youth. Listen to the shepherding chant of the Guide, who calls back whomsoever strays even a little, '**So warn them of the Day of the Imminent Event, when hearts will be in throats, choking in agony. The wrongdoers shall have no loyal friend, nor any intercessor to be obeyed.**'[32]

Separation from You is a Blaze More Intense

To the heart laid bare by love, I send my salutations,
The one scorched and seared by countless tribulations.

Grief, in its many forms, stirs in its depths,
Awakening shadows, as it relentlessly tortures.

Where can a wounded lover turn to quell this burning?
Amidst my deep longing, is there one to stoke its fire?

I bear blame for the tears that flow unchecked,
Yet in the eyes of true lovers, no such tears are kept.

Can the dove part from the rose-garden once tasting its embrace?
To endure such an abyss, is but empty heartbreak.

Why not weep for memories now veiled in the past?
The malady of love, buried deep in the chest, lasts.

32 Quran 40:18

O Soul, whose cloak of rewards has been torn into tatters by its sins. O one who has made taking the first step an abandoned path. If it concerns the Hereafter you tread lightly. If this lowly world beckons, you achieve the goal! Your aspiration for this world is in the heavens but for the next it is in the dust, and still, no sorrow grips your heart.

Eternal happiness has been attained by a people before you, who competed with one another for the Beloved. As for the wretched, each time they wish for death (in Hellfire), they are awarded ample amounts of abandonment. O people of sin, we are all embroiled in catastrophe. Is there any weeping? Any heart-wrenching pain? If you do not reconcile with your Master in these gatherings of remembrance, do you not fear the door of life being shut?

Do you seek the profits of far countries and yet, your capital is counterfeit determination? How distant are you from those that excelled? Are you not ashamed of the One who fashioned you from a clot of blood? Your aspiration for Him is frozen like winter. When will the buzzing of summer return? Or do you await shaytan to drive you to a hotter place still? These are my words of admonition with which I call out to the caravans of repentance-seekers. '**And hasten unto forgiveness from your Nurturing Lord, and for a garden whose breadth is the heavens and the earth—prepared for the pious.**'[33]

---

33 Quran 3:133

Who is Truly Mad?

Sahl ibn Abdullah al-Tustari narrates:

A man from the friends (*awliya*) of Allah, Glorified and Majestic, was beset by a strange sickness. When people would see him, they would say he has become crazy and would gang up against him. When their talk about him became too much (perhaps they felt ashamed), they said, *"We shall treat you."*

He replied, *"O people, be certain that I have a Physician. If I were to ask Him, He would heal me from every disease. However, I do not ask Him to heal me."*

They asked, *"And why is that so, when you require treatment?"*

He replied, *"I fear that if I were to be cured from this malady, I would transgress."*[34]

It was said to him, *"We have amongst us a madman, ask this physician of yours to heal him."*

"Yes, bring him to me," came his reply.

So, they brought to him a man, whose hands had been shackled to his neck in heavy chains and whose illness had possessed him. He (the pious *wali*) said to them, *"Leave me alone with him,"* and the strong amongst the men got up to loosen his chains and take him into the house. When they closed the door behind them, they thought the crazy man would do him some harm.

After some time passed, they called out and the-chained man came out to them. He replied to them intelligibly

---

34 i.e., He feared good health would make him complacent and negligent of Allah. But as long as he is unwell and frail, it helps him to recognize his weakness, humility, and dependence upon Allah. And Allah knows best.

and sanely. He was profusely weeping.

"What happened and what did you do?" The people asked him.

"I was overcome by the illness which you are aware of, not understanding anything. Then I entered upon this man, and he came closer and closer to me. He placed his hand upon my chest and another upon my head. I sensed a strange sensation spread throughout my body until the illness vanished."

"Enter his house again with us so we may ask him to beseech Allah, Glorified and Majestic, on our behalf!" They insisted.

So, he entered again with the people at his heels, but they did not find anyone in the house. Allah veiled him from the people. And whoever amongst them could reason well, had much to regret. That man was from Jerusalem and his name was Idris bin Abi Khawlah.

❁❁❁

In the sanctity of saints, is found profound truth
Is there a friend in their absence who can compare?

Friend-less, should my tears surge like a flood,
Let them flow! Let them be, till they mix with blood.

Blamers may chide, but for such love no blame,
Like a corpse to daylight, can ever take aim.

A whisper of the wind from the land they tread,
Reminds of nights with what Ahmed said.

Departed, those days, their presence not valued,
Even sleep is pained, its dreams are queued.

Deep sighs, grief of missing their meadows, assert,
Unbroken tears signal a stranded soul, lost at desert.

O rider through vast wastelands, with haste proceed
Guide through shifting sands, heed this heart's plea.

Swiftly approach, with permission enter their hallowed abode,
Deliver my greetings and stick to the road they have showed.

O seller of the most priceless of breaths for the cheapest of prices. O you who settles himself in a world in which there is no settlement. You traded everlasting profits for momentary pleasures. You did not notice you were cheated, you did not notice the outward nor inward defects in the trade. Do you show off before people in seclusion just as you do so in public?[35]

You do not walk except led by the darkness of your desires, O blind of true intuition (*baseerah*). You, who is tested with distractions, are you so eager to fulfil your lusts by lunging into fire as if you are a moth drawn to flame? Woe to you, remain in the cocoon of regret. Do not spin threads of sins over yourself and be gladdened by it. Be not like the silkworm that thinks it builds a fort around itself, but is boiled alive to harvest its silk, a quagmire of its own making.

Woe to you, if you betray the Reliever, who will relieve you? O congregation of needy ones, beautify these words and admonitions by putting them into action, who else will if not you? It is as if I can already sense the gentle breezes exhaled from the sighs of sincere hearts. O congregation of seekers, **'hasten unto forgiveness from your Nurturing Lord, and for a**

---

35 i.e., Desiring peoples' praise and admiration for ones deeds, which occurs in secrecy by wishing people observed one or practising for the moment people will observe one.

garden whose breadth is the heavens and the earth.'[36]

The Slave with Two Masters

Malik ibn Dinar narrates:

At one time, we were undergoing drought in Basra. We were going out day after day to pray for rain, but our prayers were left unanswered. Once, when I went out to pray with *Ata' al-Sulami, Thabit al-Banani, Muhammad al-Wasie', Habib al-Farasi, Salih al-Marri,* and others, we beseeched for rain but to no avail. The people returned home except *Thabit al-Banani* and I, who remained behind in the place of prayer.

When darkness fell, we noticed an African youth with thin legs and a large belly,[37] wearing two woollen garments over himself. He performed ablution, wiping over himself with a little water, and then prayed two, light cycles of prayer. Then he looked to the heavens and said, '*My Master, how often have your slaves returned to ask You, seeking something from You which holds no benefit to You. Deplete all Your reserves of water upon us! I beseech You, by Your love for me, to rain upon us this very instant!*'

He had not completed his words except that the sky burst forth and water fell down like overturned jugs. We exited from there, having to wade through water. Astonished at the youth, I turned to him and said, '*Are you not ashamed of what you said?*'

'*And what have I said?*' He asked.

---

36 Quran 3:133

37 His bloated stomach may have been a sign of malnourishment, typical of protein deficiency.

'You said – Your love for me – how do you know He loves you?' I replied.
'Do not worry about my zeal, O you whose preoccupation with his own self (nafs) has distracted him from Him,' he answered. *'Did I even exist when He favoured me with believing in His Oneness (tawheed) and in knowing Him (ma'rifa)? Do you suppose He initiated all that for me and did not love me?'* Then he briskly walked on.
'Wait, have patience with us,' I said.
'I am an owned slave,' he replied. *'I have some duties binding on me from my little master.'* He left, but I followed him until I saw him enter the house of a slave merchant.

When morning arrived, I went to the slave merchant and asked, *'Do you have a serving youth you would sell?'*
'Yes,' he replied. *'I have a hundred youths.'* He then began to present them to me, one by one.
I continued to say, *'Not that one, not that one'* until he had presented all he had. While we were walking out, I suddenly noticed the African youth, standing in a dilapidated room.
I exclaimed, *'Sell me this youth!'*
He replied, *'This is a useless boy. He has no zeal to do anything except weep.'*
'That is why I would like to buy him,' I replied.
He called the youth and said to me, *'Take him for whatever price you like, but only after you absolve me of his faults.'*
I bought him for twenty *dinars*. When we left, the youth turned to me and said, *'My master, why did you buy me?'*
'So that we could serve you,' I replied.
'Why is that?' He asked.
'Are you not our companion of last night at the place of prayer (for rain)?'

'So, you have come to know about that,' he replied.

He began to walk until he entered a mosque and performed two cycles of prayer. Then he beseeched, *'My Lord, My Master. You have disclosed the secret that was between You and I to the creation. I beseech you to take my soul this very instant!'*

And there he fell dead, may the mercy of Allah be upon him. People pray to Allah for rain, and their other needs, next to his grave to this very day.

Who can hold me back when the Beloved is near?
Who can comfort me when I am distanced?

A glance came my way, igniting my longing
It shot a killing blow to one already wounded.

Ask the winding trails upon lonely valleys
Did the Beloved smite them too, when passing by?

Ask too the visitors, what faults did they show?
That caused the Beloved to turn, somewhere else away.

O gentle breeze, from some distant shore,
You have stirred my yearning and grief once more.

Let this yearning be, for it is, indeed,
More easing to my heart that it's left be.

Beloved, remember us and remind us too,
Memory may bridge this distance anew.

Remember the days I was enriched with You,
I now drink tears and shun goblets on cue.

I was forced to gulp the bitterness of patience.
And made to drink the poison of Your absence.

In anxiety I fell, after Your separation,
As if joy was a stranger I never knew.

My Brethren, how stubbornly do you wander down the wrong path, when the right is so evident? Your ears are sealed with the wax of heedlessness, so you pay no attention to the counsel of advisors. You sold what is eternal in exchange for the temporary, having no concern over whether you profited or lost.

Woe to you, what is this insistence upon misdeeds at evening? Now it is morning, how far have the regions of old age expanded, the flag of elderliness feebly waving? How full of sin is your ledger of deeds, of scandals and wrongdoings? You are but a possession of the King of Goodness, are you not ashamed of the vile and wicked? Your entire life has been a night of heedlessness, when will we enjoy the breakfast of your awakening?

Your desires for the temporary are supported while those for the eternal are suspected. How then could your righteous deeds balance the scale of your wicked ones? Perhaps one from a distant land will reach *Arafah*, perhaps one close by will find no inclination for it. If you miss out on true repentance before death, then truly, you mourners will be in multitudes, wailing and howling at your catastrophe. Is there any other option besides repentance or righteousness from the outset? Immortality in the Hereafter is a reality but in this earthly existence, immortality is but forgery. '**Every soul shall taste death, and you will indeed be paid your rewards in full on the Day of Resurrection. And whosoever is distanced from the Fire and made to enter the Garden has certainly**

triumphed. And the life of this world is naught but the enjoyment of delusion.'[38]

The Attainment of Wisdom

Ibn Jawwad narrates:

I was sitting in (the *Masjid* of) Jerusalem (*bayt al-maqdis*) with a righteous man, when suddenly another, young man entered amongst us. Children were chasing him, throwing stones at him, and shouting out, "*Madman! Madman!*"

He entered the *Masjid*, and he was saying, "*O Allah, give me solace from this world and its abode.*"

I said to him, "*These are the words of a wise man. From where have you attained such wisdom?*"

He replied, "*Whomsoever is sincere in their service to Him, He will grant them rare wisdom and protect them through the means of preservation. I am neither crazy nor intoxicated. Rather, (I am) apprehensive and longing for Him.*" He then began to recite:

Sever your ties with all mortal beings,
Leave the crowd, you will set out for God.

Embrace patience, for it fulfills goals,
And find peace with your lot, gold or coals.

Guard well your words, let silence be your art,
For often does speech betray a believer's heart.

And struggle hard on the path to the Divine,
Roll up your sleeves, with the victorious align!

They are the chosen, the elite, the crest,
Allah's finest, His creation's very best.

---

38 Quran 3:185

With that he turned to flee. On hearing his words, I forgot this world and was left feeling sorry for him.

Alas, I see the lodges of the nurturers of hearts deserted. Where are those who would go to war with their sweet-scented tears? Where are those who would illuminate gatherings of remembrance with their breaths? Where are those whose inner-states fortified the lodges of their hearts? Where are those who would perform wonders, revealing their inner-states? Where are the hearts from where rivers of wisdom burst forth? Where are those whose hearts would shatter on mere mention of the Beloved? Do you suppose they missed the mark or is it we who are lacking in resolve to follow their way?

They painstakingly persevered, we hurry about to and fro. We slumber on the bed of heedlessness, their eyes remained awake in the dead of night. Their lofty aspirations set them apart, but how can they be recognised by those whose aspirations are confused, entangled in the temporary? Whenever their spiritual states increase in purity, ours increase in the murkiness of deprivation and deterioration. All this you will fully grasp when you settle in your graves. **'Every soul shall taste death, and you will indeed be paid your rewards in full on the Day of Resurrection. And whosoever is distanced from the Fire and made to enter the Garden has certainly triumphed. And the life of this world is naught but the enjoyment of delusion.'**[39]

---

39 Quran 3:185

O early comer to wasting time and late departer,
Until when will you deem shameful deeds good barter?

You give scant thought to Judgment Day's demand,
The day even silent limbs will take the stand.

What a wonder that truth does your gaze elude,
Instead, some crooked path comes into your view.

How this contentment in loss, sealed as your fate,
When only those who truly profit enter Heaven's gate?

The congregation of virtues is the *Ka'ba* these reminders aspire to. When its lessons are listened to and imbibed, one is buoyed up by the pure waters of its *Zamzam*.[40] Its plain of *Arafah* is the mention of those who truly know Allah (the *arifeen*). With its poetry, the rites of the virtuous (*saliheen*) are remembered. Its station of *Mina* is the desire of the repentance-seekers (*taebeen*). Its sanctuary of *khayf* [41] is reminiscence of the God-fearing ones (*kha'ifeen*). Its *maqam*[42] is the standing of the regretful ones (*nadimeen*). Its place of *sa'iy*[43] is the striving of the seekers (*salikeen*). Its *rami*[44] is the sinners casting out their sins. Its final shaving[45] is the humbling of the chiefs of the repentance-

40 Name of the well of spring water located in Mecca.

41 The Masjid of khayf is one of the Masjids of Makka, in which many pilgrims are found in the Hajj season.

42 A reference to the maqam of *Ibrahim*, or standing place of the Prophet *Ibrahim*, peace be upon him, located in front of the *Ka'ba*.

43 The ritual walk of Hajj pilgrims between *al-Safa* and *al-Marwa*.

44 The ritual throwing of stones during the Hajj pilgrimage.

45 One of the last rites of the Hajj pilgrimage is the final shaving or shortening of one's hair.

seekers (*taebeen*) – shaving some, trimming others. Its *umrah* is filling the days of the week with righteousness and its ultimate standing[46] is the blessed day of *jumuah* (Friday). Its *tawaf* [47] is the surrounding of the angels around the repentance-seekers in congratulation. The one present in it does not draw this world towards him, as he remains in the sanctuary of the penitent.

May forgiveness embrace the mere onlooker and the adamant seeker – but let the malignant envier, like *shaytan*, be wary lest they are exiled from this mosque's door. Such a one is wounded when he sees mercy descending upon another. Such a one is pained with envy when he hears eloquence and wisdom.

My Lord, after You have softened my tongue in remembrance of You, keep it hardened upon Your Oneness on the day it is most needed, O Desire of the lovers. You see me praise Your cherished ones, enumerating their virtues, yet my wage of Your forgiveness is yet to be remitted.

My Lord, I make You a reserve for the day of utmost need, for none is more impoverished than I when death descends. Cast me not aside, O Source of Goodness, O Most Generous of Benefactors!

My Lord, if I have transgressed against You with my limbs, my heart remains faithful to You. Forgive the sins of the body through the obedience of the heart.

---

46 Reference to the standing at *Arafah*, the main rite of the Hajj pilgrimage.
47 Circumambulation around the *Ka'ba*.

My Brethren, whomsoever of you has found the delight in solitary prayer, bear in mind that this work is also in need of its fair share of repentance. So let none forget this miserable soul and pray for Allah's mercy on his desolation when others forget him.

Part Three

Praise be to Allah, who, in His divinity, is far exalted above having a partner, or a deputy, or a companion, or a child. Who is far too sanctified, in His greatness, to be likened or resembled. He is the Living, the Everlasting, the Single, the Self-Sufficient. Who is so overbearing in His might, there is no adversary, no rival. Elevated in His glory, He is the One, the Unique. The heights of His sovereignty are unsurmountable, far above Him being limited to a place or a direction. He cannot, therefore, be likened, or limited. He is exalted in the Glory of His subjugating all things, far above being characterised, or consigned a form.

In His boundless mercy, He supports whom He wills, and through His justice, punishes as He deems fit. His decree upon us has been concluded so it neither halts nor hesitates. He enlivens the hearts of the intimate-knowers (*arifeen*) and puts to death the hearts of obstinate sinners. His is the verdict for the wretched, His it is for the prosperous. He renders one's final abode hidden, lost amongst His treasuries of the unseen. Yet, beneath the secret seal of death, He unveils to each slave what was written, and He revives anew.

O band of the heedless, rouse yourselves from the tradition of thoughtlessness. Realise that the pleasures of this world are passing away, while the punishment of the Hereafter is an eternal resort. By Allah, we are overwhelmed by the love of lusts but whoever amongst us succumbs to and accrues them is ruined. Know, that there is either everlasting bliss or eternal punishment.

Glorified be He who opened the inner sights of His friends to perceive deeper truths. While, alas, the hearts of the deprived have clotted. I praise Him with the praises of one shackled by sins, anxious, oscillating between fear and hope. I testify that there is no god except Allah, Alone, with no partner, a testimony I store away for 'a **day when no soul will avail another soul in any way,**'[48] and '**no parent will avail their child.**'[49] I affirm that Muhammad is His slave and Messenger, who rolled up the sleeves of hard work, toiled tirelessly for the religion of Allah, fought, and fatigued himself for its cause. May Allah bless him, his family, and companions, who against tyrants, struck steel swords.

My Brethren, when the hand of divine Power dispatched existence into being with the command, "Be!" – that is, "Be" at the door of creation, they raced to emerge. It was upon the hand of the triumphant Messenger that the signature of divine care appeared. 'Enter, O Muhammad!' For you is raised the flag of precedence! Upon the signet ring of your love is engraved, *"I was a prophet while Adam was between water and clay."*[50] O Muhammad, you are not mentioned in a book, except you embroider it and how splendidly you do so.

On the day of *Alast*[51], no gathering came together except that a covenant was made in honour of you, for a covenant was taken from the Prophets that they believe

48 Quran 2:48

49 Quran 31:33

50 Hadith, although with a weak chain.

51 The day when Allah asked all the Children of Adam, 'Am I not your Nurturing Lord?' (Alastu bi Rabbikum?). See Quran 7:172.

in you and support you.[52] The Angels, having heard of you, have since yearned to behold the one so described. Your ascension to the heavens (*al-isra*) occurred to renew your covenant and settle the yearning of those most pining of lovers.

In the whirlwind of my longing, let me be, dear friends,
Offer me solace, not censure, for where my heart tends.

I've withered in His absence, can you not see?
Alas for a moment's union to revive the spirit in me.

Let Him be the focal point of my ardent quest,
In my heart's inn, I dissolve, in His love, I rest.

Therein flows a sacred wine, my Beloved's timeless gift,
Poured in eternity, it returns to offer another sip.

This is not a wine aged in earthly barrels, nor tainted by frivolity,
But one pure and dignified, matured in the depths of spirituality.

Aged not in casks, but in the wellspring of profound belief,
Pressed long before Adam, in vessels of Divine Speech.

When you hear, "Am I not your Lord?" in those sacred tones,
It intoxicates with an age-old draught, echoing through bones.

For in the wine of God's Word, there lies triumphant life,
A victory for the soul, a balm for earthly strife.

Not like the drink of fools, who in their stupor cry,
"Pour me another barman, and leave me here to die!"

The means of travel is chosen before the journey. The axle is placed before the wheel. Likewise, Muhammad preceded creation. The Prophets are moons while he is

52 See Quran 3:81

the sun. The world is the body, he is the soul. How many a lesson he received when "**within two bows' length or nearer!**"[53] What teachings he learnt thanks to "**We shall teach you to recite, that you do not forget.**"[54] How many a secret was his heart bounded by "**at the lote tree of the boundary**"[55] and how it must have delighted. Indeed, his secret was "*if you would know what I know...*'[56]

He shared physical form with all men and said, "*I am but a man...*"[57] Yet, the tower of his felicity towered over those in the heavens and he said, "*I am not like any of you.*"[58] How evidently did the *Highest Assembly* (*al-Mala al-A'la*) know his pre-eminence when *Jibril* said to him, "*Here you are (alone) with your Lord.*"[59] And so, spread open for him was the carpet of the divine presence. He said, "*I am the master of the children of Adam on the Day of Resurrection, and I am not boasting.*"[60] His humility took its place amongst his perfect, good character for he said, "*Do not prefer me over (the Prophet) Yunus ibn Matta.*"

When he, the ascetic one of this world, entered into the monastery of "**Am I not your Nurturing Lord,**" he delighted in its intimacy. But the descent into the city of

---

53 Quran 53:9
54 Quran 87:6
55 Quran 53: 14
56 Narrated Abu Huraira: The Messenger of Allah (s) said, "If you would know what I know you would laugh little and weep much." Sahih al-Bukhari, Book 81, Hadith 74.
57 Riyad as Saliheen, 219.
58 Jami al-Tirmidhi, Book 8, Hadith 97.
59 During the Ascension or Isra of the Prophet, it is reported Gabriel said this to the Prophet when he could go no further at the 'lote tree of the boundary' and the Prophet proceeded alone.
60 Jami al-Tirmidhi, Book 49, Hadith 11.

this material world causes that delight to be evaporated, that intimacy to be replaced with the pang of separation. The roots of intimacy are pulled out. That love-sick one yearned to smell the sweet breeze from the high mountain of divine intimacy. And so, the perfumed scent diffused down to him from an ocean of goodness. His inner sight (*baseerah*) was illuminated, and he witnessed the message of the Beloved.

Overwhelmed with wonder and joy he exclaimed, "Cover me! Cover me!"[61] Saying so to trap this bliss forever within his garments. It was said – O you wrapped in garments! O you covered up! Arise and warn! Go and aid the ones crying for your help, from these souls muddied in the snare of polytheism! You are the intercessor of those to be called to account!

Your praise transcends the limits of my speech,
O noblest of Messengers, beyond what words can reach.

Endowed by Allah with Prophethood's light,
Bestowing upon you the station of unparalleled height.

Adorned in glory, in the grandest garment you stand,
A guide supreme, honour's embodiment, a guiding hand.

Your foes trembled, fear unsettling their core,
Your triumphs evident, your proofs impossible to ignore.

O jewel among creation, as the tree trunk pined for you, so did the moon yearn for you by being cleft into two, cleaving believers from disbelievers. The pebble glorified Allah in your grasp and even the lizard spoke straight to

---

61 It has been related the Prophet said this to his wife, Khadijah, after receiving the first revelation.

you. The far corners of the earth were gathered for you in the corners of your heart. For you, the desert of ascension beyond heaven was rolled up, reaching up until "**the lote tree of the boundary**" (*sidrat ul-Muntahah*).

How many showed enmity towards you but then returned to you in love? How many did fate have their hearts overturn, so animosity became religiosity? The worship of the Prophets reached its zenith when you led them in prayer in unearthly realms. Your message's beauty was unveiled in the union of the night journey (*isra*) on the stage of "**within two bows' length or nearer,**" so that the heavenly assembly, those that once questioned, "**Will you place someone therein,**"[62] could witness the unrivalled pearl of creation, buried in the shell of Adam. Even the chief of the Angels partook in your teachings, inquiring, *"O Muhammad…What is Islam? What is faith (imaan)? What is excellence (ihsan)?"* The noblest of the *jinn* journeyed to verify your religion saying, "**Truly we have heard a wondrous Qur'an.**"[63] The best of men accompanied you, that intimate one, "**the second of the two whilst in the cave.**"[64]

If the day's sun reveals hidden, material things, then the sun of your religion (*shariah*) unveils the unseen, for you said, *"Beware of the insight of the believer for he sees with the*

---

62 "**And when your Lord said to the angels, "I am placing a vicegerent upon the earth," they said, "Will you place someone therein who will work corruption, and shed blood, while we hymn Thy praise and call Thee Holy?" He said, "Truly I know what you know not.**" - Quran 2:30

63 Quran 72:1

64 Quran 9:41. i.e., Abu Bakr Siddeeq, may Allah be pleased with him.

light of Allah."[65] How few are the guiding stars guiding wayward travellers compared to the stars of your proofs guiding to reality. Do not wonder at the Messengers saying, *"Myself! Myself!"*[66] Our Prophet, Muhammad, peace and blessings be upon him, will offer his self to another self in need. His plea not for himself, but *"My nation! My nation!"* O Allah, how sweet is this beloved one's reminiscence!

The one who faults me for my love, they wrong me deep,
To the fruits of my painful longing, let me reap.

In dreams, his form appears, a vision soft and clear,
And in the wakeful night, his memory draws near.

Every inch of my being testifies to love's profound embrace,
This truth alone is enough; no further inquiry has its place.

With every surge of yearning, I longed for his sight,
Alas, my life! Lost in longing, day, and night.

Never had I seen the dawn's early light so clear,
Until this radiant sun among men did appear.

How many a deceiver, coming to delude, did he dazzle. On beholding his moon-like face men would exclaim, *"This is not the face of a liar!"*[67] While the beauty of *Yusuf* captivated women, how amazing is our Prophet who enchants the heavens and earth! How numerous were those healed by his mere saliva! No nation of any Prophet was crowned with anything more honourable than his nation, donning the crown of "**You are the best community brought forth**

65 Hadith, al-Tirmidhi, Book 47, Hadith 179.

66 i.e., on the Day of Judgement. See Hadith, Riyad as-Salihin Book 18, Hadith 59.

67 Hadith, al-Tirmidhi, Book 37, Hadith 71

unto mankind..."[68] No companion of any Prophet was given a mantle like his Companions, that of "**Those who are with him are relentless against the disbelievers, merciful to one another.**"[69] In the mosques of their nights, the Companions were like monks in fervent prayer. By day, they stood like warriors united together. Such they were described, "Monks by night, warriors by day."

My Lord, I cannot fathom that You would ever sever the hope of one whose tongue you have let loose with Your Oneness (*tawheed*) and praise upon Your messenger.

My Lord, as You have appointed the Prophet a guide to You, make remembrance of him a means to reach You.

My Lord, how immense are Your blessings upon us, having guided us through the Seal of the Prophets.

My Lord, by the nearness of the one You have drawn near in intimate knowledge (*ma'rifa*), draw us closer to Your forgiveness and mercy, O Most Merciful of those who show mercy.

---

68 Quran 3:110
69 Quran 48:29

Part Four

The praise belongs to Allah, who makes affairs flow to the course of His will, in the succession of night and day. He crafted creation and set it in order with the utmost excellence. Glorified be He, beyond any imperfection, the Ordainer of Decrees. He ordained as He willed and disposes as He wills. "**And your Nurturing Lord creates what He wills, and He chooses; no choice have they.**"[70] He predetermined every creation before its existence, and the pen has dried having inscribed the decree. He rotates the heavenly bodies, embedding in them the secrets that oblige them to obey heavenly laws, marking the passage of time. His wisdom is manifest in existence and in its prevailing order. He devised every astonishing aspect, inviting hearts and minds to explore its depths.

He created the pen and said to it, "Write with My power what My will dictates!" And it wrote each being's sustenance, its portion of good character,[71] its span of life, and its moments of joy and sorrow. He created the Preserved Tablet (*al-Lawh al-Mahfooz*) to preserve His secrets, yet still made it subject to change.[72] He crafted His throne with the curious qualities of perfection and distinction. He rose above (*istiwa'*) His throne, but He is

---

70 Quran 28:68

71 "Allah Almighty allotted character between you as He divided provision between you. Allah Almighty bestows wealth on those He loves and those He does not love. He only bestows faith upon those who He loves...." – Hadith, Al-Adab Al-Mufrad, Imam Bukhari, Book 14, Hadith 275.

72 "Nothing but supplication averts the decree, and nothing but righteousness increases life." Hadith, Miskat al-Masabih, Book 9, Hadith 11.

beyond physical settlement. He fashioned bodily forms as an arena for souls, believers triumphant and deniers, lost. He established the oft-frequented house (*bayt al-mamour*) for angelic pilgrimage and frequented it with mysteries. He created the "**the lote tree of the boundary**" (*sidrat ul-Muntahah*), its compassionate leaves are like shades from Hellfire. It is the destination sought by spiritual seekers, travelling towards His presence of beauty and light. The heavens He layered and invited in the angels, the disposers of His decrees. He formed the earth and populated it with the "two handfuls" – a handful for paradise and another to be tossed to Hell. Glorified be He, Who compels all things that have beginning, while He, alone, is Beginningless. Glorified be He, whose divinity prevents minds from grasping Him. I praise Him, even though I have been retired by procrastination, and am left weeping among ruined debris.

I testify that there is no deity, save Allah, Alone, and without partner – a testimony I cling to for a Day when burdens will be loaded. I testify that Muhammad is His slave and messenger, the selected one, the elected, the chosen. May the peace and blessings of Allah be upon him, and his family, and companions – a prayer that I keep for a Day when veils will be unveiled.

When Allah, be He glorified, filled the spread-out earth for the nurturing of His creation, the heavens boasted of its greatness over it. The earth bowed its head in humility and stretched forth the hand of poverty saying, "I only beg from the Rich One Beyond All Existence." In response, He generously provided rebuttals for the heavens' arrogance.

O heavens! If you boast of the sun for its illumination of material forms, then the sun of the *shariah* of Muhammad, peace and blessings of Allah be upon him, illuminates the Unseen World (*ghayb*). The sun of your skies sets, but the sun of the *shariah* of Muhammad does not set. If you boast of the beauty of the moon and its brilliance, then it is eclipsed by the beauty of his radiant visage and light, peace and blessings of Allah be upon him, and he is not eclipsed.[73] Amidst the apprehension of your eclipses, prayers are accepted from the people of earth, and the one who supplicates is better than things that are supplicated for!

Or do you take pride in your stars, guiding travellers on sea and land? But the Companions of our Prophet are *"like stars; whoever amongst them you use for guidance, you are guided."*[74] And if you are fortified with "**lamps made as missiles against devils,**"[75] then here walked *Umar*, may Allah be pleased with him, who poked the eye of *shaytan* and burned him with the flame of his faith. For *Umar* never walked a path, but *shaytan* would walk another, giving him a wide berth.

If you take pride in the Preserved Tablet (*al-lawh al-mahfooz*), inscribed by a created pen, then here, hearts are inscribed directly with the hand of the Creator's Power, "**Allah has inscribed faith upon their hearts.**"[76]

---

73 Jabir ibn Samura narrates, "I saw Allah's Messenger (Allah bless him and give him peace) on a cloudless night, and he was wearing a red suit of clothes, so I started looking at him and then at the moon. Indeed, I found him more beautiful than the moon." - Hadith, Ash-Shama'il al-Muhammadiyah, Book 1, Hadith 9.

74 Hadith , Musnad ibn Humayd, Hadith 1027.

75 Quran 67:5

76 Quran 58:22

If you are proud because you surround the vastness of His podium (*kursi*), how do you compare to the vastness of a human's heart, for He says *"The heart of My believing slave encompasses Me."*[77] And if you are proud of Angel *Israfil's* blowing of the trumpet to revive souls into bodies then how does that compare to His blowing of faith into our hearts, illuminating them till the Day of Judgement?

If you take pride in the unending rows of angels and their glorifications, then how many here have been described as "**an upright community who recite Allah's signs in the watches of the night, while they prostrate,**"[78] standing on the feet of hope? How many a window is opened in the late of night, of lovers of Allah seeking forgiveness?

If you boast of the compassion of Angel *Mika'il* and his modesty, then we have *Abu Bakr* and how many cities flourished with the compassion of *Abu Bakr*? And if you boast of the strength of Angel *Jibril* and his resoluteness, then the earth claims *Umar* and his resoluteness on the day he embraced faith, saying, *"By Allah, Allah will not be worshipped secretly after this day whilst Umar is alive!"* He strode valiantly towards the *Ka'ba,* dispelling adversity from Islam.

If you boast of drops of water that revive dead vegetation, then how do you compare to the flowing of tears that revives dead hearts? How many a heart bounded by a body is grander than the "lote tree of the boundary"

---

77 Hadith mentioned by Imam al-Ghazali in his Ihya uloom al-din.

78 Quran 3:113

(*sidrat ul-muntaha*)!

If you boast that paradise is within you, then paradise itself waits to welcome the believers in its embrace. The angels will be their attendants, rushing towards them "**from every gate. 'Peace be upon you because you were patient.'**"[79] The angels initiate greetings desiring to hear return greetings from the people of Paradise, and to set eyes upon them. Such are the stations of the righteous, those blessed with the treasure of sincerity. All the while, the angels, "**seek forgiveness for those who believe.**"[80]

If you take pride in the divine throne and those that revolve around it, then where do you stand compared to the *Ka'ba* and those that revolve around it? Where is your black stone, connected so deeply with the fates of men since the day of *Alast*?

When Adam descended to earth to take upon himself the vicegerency of Allah (*khalifah*), he found this kingdom was already prepared for his arrival, and the sanctuary of the *Ka'ba* decorated. Donning the *ihram*[81] is a means to seek divine help, and the standing at *Arafah* is a door through which the beggar enters to receive his wish. When the *Ka'ba* was built, Allah commanded His friend, *Ibrahim*, upon him be peace, to give the call to His house on the honoured mountain of *Abu Qubays*. He said, "*My Nurturing Lord, will my call reach anyone?*"

---

79 Quran 13:23-24
80 Quran 40:7
81 The state a pilgrim enters when performing hajj or umrah. In which, one shows their humility to Allah by observing certain restrictions.

It was said, *"O Ibrahim, the call is from you, its communication is from Us."*[82] When his call passed through the sacred, black stone, it stirred all those destined to perform *hajj* to respond. They crowded at the door of acceptance, their flag being *"Labbayk, Allahumma labbayk"* (*Here we are at Your service O Lord, here we are*).

The Grand Vizier

One day, the vizier of *Harun al-Rashid, Abdullah ibn Masrooq*, sat before the caliph and said, *"O Commander of the Believers, if a man sought your help in returning a runaway slave that was with you, would you not return the slave?"*
Harun al-Rashid replied, *"Of course."*
Ibn Masrooq replied, *"Then I am the runaway slave of Allah. Release me so I can return to His service for I desire to return."*
Harun al-Rashid and those with him wept profusely and he said, *"This man has succeeded where we have failed,"* releasing *Ibn Masrooq* from his position.
Abdullah ibn Masrooq entered into the state of *ihram* for pilgrimage, saying *"labbayk Allahumma labbayk"* (Here I am at Your service O Lord, here I am). On the way, *Sufyan al-Thawri* came across him, sleeping on the earth and the wind blowing dirt all over him. *Sufyan* greeted him and asked, *"O Abdullah, what has Allah given you in exchange for what you gave up?"*
He replied, *"O Sufyan, I have been given contentment in my heart for whatever state I find myself in."*

Ibn Masrooq then proceeded to Mecca. When the elders of Mecca heard of his imminent arrival, they set out to greet him. On seeing the coarseness of his state and his

82 Ibn Kathir mentions this hadith in his tafsir to verse 22:27.

exhaustion from his journey they questioned him, *"How do you feel about the coarseness of your state, your exhaustion, and your having to endure the vast desert?"*
He replied, *"And how else does a disobedient slave return to the house of his Master? By Allah, if I could, I would slither to Him on my face."* He then began to weep profusely.
"Why such weeping?" they asked him.
"I hope it will intercede for me, perhaps He will accept my repentance," he replied, causing all those present to weep.

When his eyes fell upon the *Ka'ba,* he fell where he stood and could not be revived. May the mercy of Allah be upon him.

When the camels heard the chanting of divine love and care, they became engrossed with joy. They tired their bodies racing forth[83] and stretched out their necks to embrace the angels on arrival at the sacred house. How amazing how they partake in **"and they bear your burdens to a land you would never reach, save with great hardship to yourselves."**[84]

Tread gently, O cameleer, as she hastens her pace!
Does the sight of the Black Stone not grace her face?

Does not our Shariah teach mercy, oh how true –
But for worldly chases, her joints you've wearied through.

Though you may guide her reins on this earthly trail,
The Divine Decree-er owns her life, upon which you sail.

83 Camels are known to hasten their trot when hearing chants from their cameleers.
84 Quran 16:7

In showing her kindness, your aims you'll achieve,
For he who tends with gentleness will likewise receive.

The hajj voyage fills her with a yearning so profound,
See how she sways, lost in dreams that know no bound!

If the camel's heart shows more yearning than yours,
Then you are indeed deserving of deep sympathy.

Sixty Pilgrimages

Ali ibn Muwaffaq narrates:
When I had completed sixty pilgrimages, I told myself I will now stay at home and rest. I heard a voice coming from the *Ka'ba* saying, *"O Ibn Muwaffaq! If We had not loved you, We would not have invited you here!"* Hearing that, I got up and began repeating *labbayk, Allahumma labbayk* (Here I am O Lord, at Your service. Here I am). Then I said, *"My Nurturing Lord, I make you witness that the rewards for all my (extra) pilgrimages be dedicated to Muhammad, peace and blessings of Allah be upon him, his Companions, and all the Muslims!"*

When I later stood at *Arafah,* and saw the masses humbling themselves in supplications, I said, *"My Nurturing Lord, if you have accepted my pilgrimage and there is here anyone whose pilgrimage You have not accepted, then let this pilgrimage of mine be dedicated to them."*

Then I heard a voice saying, *"O Ibn Muwaffaq! Do you intend to show generosity greater than Mine? By My Honour and Majesty, I have forgiven all the people of Arafah, and on top of that, everyone from their families, and I am the Oft-Forgiving, Most Merciful."*

Know that to fulfill your covenants is part of faith. So, renew your commitment to the covenant made on the day of *Alast*. My Brethren, mentioning these places causes a yearning in the heart, as if they are woven into one's very being. O you dead of feeling! When shall we see you amongst the righteous travellers responding? How strange that my admonishment shakes the branches, but the fruits of your awakening do not fall. Has the tree of your heart withered and rotted? How tragic if both the fruit and tree be lost. Woe to a body devoid of a soul. How lamentable that the camel responds passionately to the cameleer's chant, but you remain rigid to the meanings of this song.

My Lord, we have drunk from the cup of admonition, but are perhaps sidetracked with the allure of beholding Your earthly blessings. My Lord, by the sanctity of the one you make reach Your sanctity, do not withhold Your support from those imprisoned in the dungeon of disobedience. Have mercy upon us by the one You have accepted through Your overflowing grace, O Most Merciful of those who show mercy.

Part Five

The praise is due to Allah who has shrouded the secrets of His decrees from the grasp of minds, so that one desirous to unveil them has no hope. He has subdued existent things with the blemish of needing a beginning, everything other than Him is weak and dependent.

He humbled kings with the flaw of misfortunes, the anguish of loss, and unceasing calamities. Their castles, once the epitome of luxury, now bask in ruins. Where their strength was once united, now is scattered amongst the fragments of imaginations. Their advisors and aides could not aid them, their followers offered no support. The hand of adversity toyed with them, their companions grew weary of their company, and those driven by desire and ambition deserted them.

Alas! I wonder, are those laid to rest in the depth of the earth delighted with their new abodes that they do not return, or are they forbidden from returning? News about them has vanished, their traces erased, and their loved ones sip the cup of misfortune. By Allah, how many drink from the glass of grief, alone in the darkness of their graves, until their drink became tears? They yearned for just an hour's return. What a distant hope! The journey of death is a one-way ride.

Allah bless the hearts of His intimate devotees (*arifeen*) who lament the passing of the days of youth, whose tears flow copiously for missed opportunities of righteous deeds. O you, who have been removed from Allah's door by your sins, mourn your time of exile and return. Those struck with fear, with flowing tears and apprehensive hearts, are surely welcomed at the Master's threshold.

Glorified be He, Who has tarnished the pleasures of this world for those who seek them, has clouded their vision, and dulled their hearing. I praise Him, with the praise of one who acknowledges the allotment of His decree. Some seek Him out, others stray from His path, and yet others return to Him in repentance.

I testify that there is no deity except Allah, Alone, and with no partner – a testimony I deposit with One who does not misplace what is entrusted to Him. And I testify that Muhammad, whom He dispatched, is His slave and messenger, whose message's light shines brightly. May the peace and blessings of Allah be upon him, his family, and companions each time the gentle breeze blows and bird songs waft from lush branches.

My Brethren, what escape is there from the irrational impulsiveness of the mind, and what means is there to avoid the fickleness of the heart? Oh, if only I knew what has robbed you of the shirt of obedience! How often must the days repeat the lesson that all that is built up returns to rubble? How often do the harbingers of white hair need to foreshadow the looming shadow of your gravestone? All the while you remain preoccupied with the profession of heedlessness. Do you purchase your worldly desires with abundant coins yet offer faith merely a meagre tax? How often are you visited by the emissaries of death, reinforcing that you shall remain only a bit longer after the passing of others? Woe to you if you dirty the dress of your faith with the filth of this world such that on the Day when others appear adorned, you find no garment to wear.

When emotions reign, the mind cracks and acts contrary to wisdom. For the mind should judge and validate emotion, but when roles are reversed, the repercussions are swift and severe. Should one weigh the fleeting joy of worldly pleasures against their ensuing sorrow, the latter would surely outweigh the former. If you are preoccupied with preparing your sons and daughters for this world, when will you prepare yourself for the world of the grave? Wail over yourself before others wail over you. Weep before you are wept over.

O you, who finds this earthly abode agreeable, tears of your repentance should flow, yet you remain oblivious. How could you betray righteous deeds when they are sincere companions? When will I see your desires put to trial by the judge of self-restraint? When will you ready the arrows of determination to target the victory of hitting your true purpose? Oh, how I wish to know where are those whose wisdom conquered their hearts! Alas, our inner vision has been blinded from witnessing what they witness. But if we should meet their qualities, we would likely flee, as if we are opposites that are not united.

Our heart's vision is blinded to what the insightful see. How dark becomes a home after its occupants depart, how lonely a building after its dwellers have moved on. Is there in this gathering one to weep with me? Is there one who's ears pay heed?

My Brethren, each day is a station we stop at, and the first stop to the Hereafter is the grave. From that first moment you stepped out of the refuge of the womb to this desert of the world, you have been voyaging, but the heedless one takes no provisions on his journey. For how much longer will you squander this priceless jewel of life for a petty price? When will your mind stand tested in the court of repentance? When will you gather the riches of reason from the tears of wisdom, to spend on the necessities of righteous deeds?

Woe to you, extend your palms for the charity of guidance, deep in the depths of the ocean of night, perhaps the pearl of response will be found. Or would you rather lose your time in futile pursuits?

Woe to a back that will break but not satisfy its stomach. Woe to a morsel that induces groans of punishment. If the bird is overcome by its love of seeds, it falls into the trap! If would suffice you to concern yourself with what you have been created for.

The Keeper of the Blind

It has been recounted that a man attended a funeral prayer with *Abu Bakr al-Dhareer* (the Blind). At the front of the funeral, were some boys weeping and lamenting, *"Who remains for us after you, dear father!"* Their words were conveyed to *Abu Bakr al-Dhareer* and after the funeral prayer was concluded, he was asked about his thoughts regarding the boys' lamentation.

He replied with saying, *"I remember my father was very old and poor. One night, I overheard him talking to my mother, 'I am very old and poor, as are you. Oh! Everyone must work for their bread, so what will happen to this young, blind son of ours!' Upon that my father wept, and it grieved my heart.*

The following morning, as was my routine, I headed to the Quran school. A little while later, a servant of the caliph's mother arrived and asked the teacher, 'Has she (the caliph's mother) not told you that Ramadan is approaching, and she would like a young boy with excellent Quranic recitation to recite to her?'

The teacher said to me, 'You should go, O Abu Bakr.' The servant took me to the castle of the caliph, and then into her quarters. I greeted her with salaam respectfully and began my recitation. She began to weep profusely, and I too was overcome with tears.

She asked me why I was crying, and I recounted the conversation I had overheard between my father and mother the previous night. Her tears flowed even more, and she ordered that I be given a thousand gold dinars, a fine robe, a mule with an ornate saddle, and an additional monthly allowance of a hundred silver dirhams. I returned to my father's house with these gifts."

How strange! Do I cry out aloud only to find no one will shed a tear? How much shall I speak to witness no result? If the springs of eyes have dried up, how can any expression of mine succeed? Whoever reaches the shores of regret and remorse – they shall see abundant tears. And whosoever mourns their wasted past, will be engulfed with the waves of repentance-inducing sorrow.

My Lord! Open for us the doors of Your gentleness. Open for us what will open the way of Your obedience. My Lord, revive the parched hearts of the repentance-seekers with the downpour of Your acceptance. My Lord, make us from amongst those You have sent down the path of "**There is no blame on the good-doers.**"[85] My Lord, soothe us with the waters of Your forgiveness until the fires of our lusts are put out! My Lord, make our desires aligned with Your obedience, O Most Merciful of those that show mercy!

---

85 Quran 9: 91

Part Six

The praise belongs to Allah who brings the clouds to tears, thereby coaxing flowers to smile, and the cheeks of gardens to become rosy with hues of red, yellow, white, and black. Meadows beam with an array of greenery, a visage delighting sights and minds, while the gentle breeze's fingertips softly caress their branches. The singers of the birds call out to each other in response. The bulbul's song is like a flute's, the ringdove joins in harmony, and the nightingale delivers its chorus. Tree limbs fall into hypnotic dance, clapping their leaves in lively applause, all the while the blowing gale puts instruments to shame. The reaching roots of the cactus make way for water, uniting in celebration at channels and rivers.

Spring adorns rich forests gilded with green, treasured saffron above and likely gold below. It entices the branches to let down their locks of leaves, knitting upon them threads of blossoms. Fine balance and exquisite taste merge, leaving the foremost artists dazed in the delight of perfection being achieved! The embroideries on spring's robe are embellished, thus rendering exquisite the spectacle of existence. The finely-tuned balance of night and day wards off monotony. So completely does this world captivate, for it men will lose their minds, and women, their hearts.

On still nights, the gentle breeze quietly opens a vial of flowery fragrance, earthly incense, and pure musk. By morning, rows of roses are neatly arranged, and elegance prances down well-trodden paths carved by tears on the cheeks of longing gardens. Ah! How splendid is this life – if not for the looming swallow of death and trading all above the earth for the drowning darkness beneath it!

Those who know Allah strive for eternal deeds, and abstain from fleeting living, for they understand its joys are momentary and do not last. How excellent are the intimate-knowers (*arifeen*) who forbid slumber to their eyes, and out of their eagerness, make their nights like their days.

Glorified be He, who infused the breaths of His intimate-knowers with the musk of *ma'rifa* (knowledge of Him), and the perfume of attentiveness. I praise Him with the praise of one whose sins have distanced him from His door. I draw near, kissing the dirt with the lips of hope.

I testify that there is no deity except Allah, Alone, without partner – a testimony I prepare on the path of the righteous and spiritual elite. I testify that Muhammad is His slave and messenger, whom He sent when the sewerage of disbelief had polluted the river of faith, and so Allah restored His message like He illuminates the day. May the peace and blessings of Allah be upon Muhammad, his family, and his companions, every time the seeker breathes in the air of late night prayer.

When the winds of Allah's care began to stir from the sanctuary of His protection, the clouds of compassion began to sail, sending down torrents of admonition and warning upon the dirt on the hearts of the repentant. Their bodies were shaken into service and were strengthened with steadfast perseverance, until flowers of forgiveness blossomed on their faces. The pods of their tongues opened, releasing the nectar of remembrance (*dhikr*), the birds of profound knowledge sang on the branches of their wisdom, and their scales of repentance grew weighty with wails of their regret.

The myrtle of contentment, the water lily of loyalty, and the daffodil of faithfulness all diffused their scents, as well as the jasmine of removing one's reliance on creation. The rose of love beamed and the windflower of inner peace shone over the crystal waters of remembrance, from which flowed tears of remorse. The yarrow,[86] fragranced with contentment with divine decree, and the narcissus of submission spread their aromas. Thus, the barren soil of the sinner's heart transformed into a garden of repentance beneath the watchfulness of divine direction. The tongues of the knowing ones echoed, "**Among His signs is that you see the earth diminished; then, when We send down water upon it, it quivers and swells. He Who gives it life is surely the One Who gives life to the dead. Truly He is Powerful over all things.**"[87]

When tear drops fell from the clouds of eyes onto the earth of cheeks, flowers of godly fear emerged, scenting their breaths with the fragrance of contemplating Allah (*muraqaba*). The wells of their hearts, filled with divine love, echoed melodies from the branches of infatuation with Allah alone. Stones of yearning sparked the fire of longing in the hearth of their hearts, and their moments of *muraqaba* became clear of the clouds of heedlessness. Here, appeared signs of the beauty of the Beloved, and

86 A tall, flowering plant.
87 Quran 41:37

minds raced in attempts to behold Him! The preacher has done well, but where are those possessed with hearing?

Keeping an Eye on One's Spiritual State

It has been mentioned from *Amr bin Malik* that his father said:

I had a special brotherhood with *Ali bin al-Musamiri*. When he passed away, may the mercy of Allah be upon him, I wished to see him in a dream. I ended up seeing him in a beautiful form, yet with one eye closed. I said to him, *"My brother, I left you in this world knowing full well that there was no pain nor problem with your eye. Why is one of your eyes now closed?"*

He replied, *"While I was in the world, I was reciting the Book of Allah, Glorified and Majestic, one night. I passed by a verse of divine warning and one of my eyes wept, but the other did not.*

I lost consciousness and when I awoke, I said to my dry eye, 'What is the matter with you that you do not aid me in weeping! I swear by my Beloved Lord, if He fulfils my hope and allows me to behold Him, I will prevent you from looking at Him!'

When I met my Beloved Master, He said to me, 'O Ali, here I am. Delight in the vision of My Noble Countenance.' And so, I shut my tearless eye, fulfilling my earlier pledge."

What a wonder that such is the contemplation of the devout, and despite you contemplating many a calamity, your hearts are still drawn to this world. For the righteous, the dawn of the hereafter and reunion has drawn close, and so they fastened their pace. Yet here you squat in gloomy squalor.

O gathering of seekers, lower the sight of your hearts from this world's insignificance by truly contemplating Allah with vigilance. Hold back the steps of your missteps in this arena of worldly desires. For the One who scrutinises you is the All-Seeing. Sheathe those arrows of backbiting, do not make a target out of the honours of men and women. How often does a bullet rebound upon its shooter? How many a word wounds its speaker? How often a look removes the spiritual sight of the gazer! How often have you belittled a little sin, when a mosquito killed Nimrod, and a pellet drops an elephant? When absolute power belongs to Another, do you think caution alone will help? When your success lies in the hands of Another, can mere effort be of any benefit?

How Often the Weak Amaze the Strong

Abu al-Hassan al-Darrah relates:

One year, I embarked for Hajj alone. Upon entering the masjid of *Qadisiya*, I saw a disabled man at its *mihrab*. I greeted him with *salaam*, and he responded. He asked, *"O Abu al-Hassan, have you resolved upon performing hajj this year alone?"*

"Yes," I replied.

"Accompany me," he said.

I thought to myself that I have escaped from my companions to travel alone, shall I now accompany a disabled man! So, I replied, *"No."*

"Do so," he persisted.

"By Allah, I will not do so."

He answered with, *"May Allah show kindness on the weak*

that will leave the strong in wonder."

I left him and proceeded for the next gathering point, arriving at mid-morning the next day. I entered the masjid there and was amazed to find the disabled *shaykh* sitting at its *mihrab*! I greeted him with *salaam* and he replied to my greeting and said, *"O Abu al-Hassan, May Allah show kindness on the weak until the strong wonder!"*

I was left amazed at him but nevertheless proceeded until I reached the gathering point of *Fira'a* the next morning. I entered its masjid, and there was the *shaykh* again sitting inside! He said to me the same words he said the day before. I sat down as his feet and said, *"My master, pardon me. Perhaps I can accompany you?"*
He replied, *"By Allah, I would dislike that you break your oath (to travel alone)."* Then he left me and headed on.
By Allah, I met him again at the gathering place near the city of Muhammad, peace and blessings of Allah be upon him. Then I lost sight of him again.

On arriving at Mecca, I mentioned him to a gathering that included *Abu Bakr al-Kattani, Sariya al-Saqti,* and *Abu al-Hassan al-Muzni*. They considered me a fool saying, *"That is Abu Jafar al-Majzoub! He is one upon whom the signs of Allah are visible and is of high spiritual states. There is not one among us except that he wishes that Allah will allow meeting him! We hope if you see him again that you gain his favour so that we may also meet him."*
I kept an eye out for him and on the day of Eid I felt a tugging from behind and someone saying, *"Peace be upon you, O Abu al-Hassan."*

I looked back, and it was the shaykh! He said, *"Send my greetings to Abu Bakr al-Kattani, Sariya al-Saqati, and their group."* I marvelled at his words that were as if he was amongst us during our conversation.

O Turner of Hearts, turn our hearts upon Your obedience so that we submit to You and You accept us. O Reliever of calamities, open for us a door from the doors of Your forgiveness so that the garden of Your kindness be opened before us, O Most Merciful of those that show mercy!

Part Seven

The praise belongs to Allah, who conjures creation from the abyss of nonexistence. He made guidance a means of joy for the one He guided. He leads astray the one who is disgraced in His knowledge. He devised divine decree in the mother of books (*um al-Kitab*) and manifested it by means of the Tablet (*al-Lawh al-Mahfooz*) and the Pen. He turns celestial bodies in circles with the power of His dominance, and through their revolutions, displays darkness and light. Minds are incapable of encapsulating His essence, and no foot steps foot in His courtyard. He made existent things signposts pointing to His power, raising them like banners to beholders. His overflowing generosity flows down to all worlds, showering them with abundant blessings.

He veiled the inner sight of the heedless from the evidences of contemplation, but explained them plainly for the eager. He denied those impoverished from seeking the goal of the Hereafter, where then can the forsaken find refuge when He passes His judgement? He brought into His presence the hearts of the *arifeen* without medium or physical movement.

He is the Giver of life, Bringer of death, He guides aright, He leads astray, He honours, He disgraces, He bestows, and He withholds. There is none to fend off His command, nor one to undo what He weaves, nor resist what He decrees. He plants the feet of the diligent in the darkness of night to stand in prayer. He selects them as recipients of His friendship and elevates them as people of virtue and lofty endeavour. He watches over them with the sword of His protection and has praised them since before time. For the Glorious states in His clear, precious book, "**...and that He may reward those who did good with what is most beautiful.**"[88]

Glorified be He who knows the secrets of final endings, from the first to the last. I praise Him with the praise of one incapable of gratitude for the copious blessings He bestowed. I testify that there is no deity except Allah, Alone, no partner has He, a testimony that I hope to seal the scroll of my deeds with when it is wrapped up. I testify that Muhammad is His slave and messenger, dispatched to all nations. May the peace and blessings of Allah be upon him, his family, and his companions, at each instance of darkness giving way to light.

My Brethren, why this complacency? Pry open the shells of hearing and pay heed. Perhaps the drops of this sermon may crystallise into pearls of repentance. How often has the merchant of preaching displayed the riches of the Hereafter only to find no buyer! How often does the fragrance of encouragement waft toward you, but the deluded lose their sense of smell due to the sickness of heedlessness and holding fast to false hopes. Such a one pursues mirages and returns back parched.

How peculiar that you find this world's water sweet, while those who can truly discern, find it bitter. Your illness distorts your palate, making heedlessness delectable. When varieties of good deeds are presented before you, none appeal to your taste. The doctor checked the beating of your heart for abstinence but found no pulse.

---

88 Quran 53:31

Your limbs of worshipful acts have dried their tears and consoled each other. As for the hearts of the penitent, they are like the olive "**whose oil would almost glow.**"[89] And whosoever drinks from the cup of friendship with the Beloved, their joy never ends.

Whoever desires material wealth, loses it at death. Whoever finds solace in worldly comforts, will have to make do with entombment. Wealth is only what is eternal, these temporary trinkets are but counterfeit.
When this lowly world is remembered your heart is moved onward. When the Hereafter is mentioned, your resolve resigns at the doorstep. Your steed of good deeds slips where it steps. Your heart's vision is clouded with cataract. Your horse has no horsepower. Can you expect to catch up to the rear of the caravan of the righteous?

Umar ibn al-Khattab would be prone to knock the door of *Huthayfa ibn al-Yaman*, may Allah be pleased with them both, in the middle of the night, tearful and asking, *"O Huthayfa, I implore you by Allah. The Messenger of Allah, peace and blessings of Allah be upon him, charged you with the names of the hypocrites. Did he include the name of Umar amongst them?"*
To which *Huthayfa* wept and replied, *"No, by Allah."*
Yet *Umar* would say, *"I know you to be truthful in speech, but my deeds resemble those of the hypocrites…"*
Such were the righteous, yet you are unaware. O you whose body is amongst us, where has your heart flown off to?

My Brethren, come, let us weep over our plight, for our

89 Quran 24:35

grief is one. Do you know how others have profited while you have lost? They had no long winding hopes for this world, rather their hopes were as brief as their breaths. Their sleep was lighter than a doze. Their late nights in prayer were sweeter than the embrace of a loved one. The late night breeze was their perfume, their eyes overflowing like fountains. Their zeal was their worry for what would become of them after death. Their gardens bloomed with pious acts. Their fervour was composed of earnest efforts. Their breaths were scented with wise words. Such are the traits of the virtuous, make do with them as exemplars.

Signs of Love

One of the *arifeen* narrates:
I once observed a lover with their beloved. As they were talking, I noticed the beloved one verbally insulting their lover. The lover was lowering their head, humbled, responding in a soft and kind manner, sometimes kissing the beloved's hand, sometimes their foot.

I was amazed at what was occurring between them. I turned away, still pondering them in my heart. I then happened upon a group of Sufis and mentioned what I had witnessed between that lover and their beloved. Amongst them was a truthful seeker (*faqir*) who let out a loud cry and started to weep until he lost consciousness. When he came around, he was asked about his reaction to which he said, *"I was struck by that lover's reverence and that beloved's pride. It roused the heart-break in my heart, renewed the sighs of love (for Allah), ashamed me for my shortcomings, objections, false claims, and excessive heedlessness. Thus, I was overcome by the state which you witnessed."*

My Brethren, the diligent have drawn near, while we have distanced ourselves. The righteous have arrived, we have abandoned the path. They have been graced with spiritual states, we have been denied. They have been rescued from the destruction of desires, we have succumbed to them. They attained the objective, we have lost it. They wear the garment of faith, we have been deprived of it. So come, my Brethren, let us weep for ourselves and lament our plight. I hope this sentence of exile from the Beloved nears its end.

Allah is the Only Hope

Malik ibn Dinar narrates:

I saw a funeral procession that was not being followed by anyone except one man. I said, *"A funeral and only one person partakes in it!"* It was said that the deceased was a sinner, guilty, and excessive in wrongdoing. That was why no one would partake in his funeral prayer.

I prayed over him and placed him in his grave. I then wandered over to the shade of a nearby tree. I was overcome by sleep and dreamt that there were suddenly two angels that descended. One of them said to the other, *"Examine his two eyes."*

The other replied, *"He has never looked at any goodness with them."*

"Examine his two ears."

"He has never heard any goodness with them."

"Examine his two hands."

"He has never stretched them towards any good."
"Examine his two legs."
"He has never walked with them towards any good."
"Look to his heart."
The angel looked a long while, then said to his companion, *"My brother, I see his heart filled with the Oneness of Allah (tawheed)."*
The other replied, *"Write him from amongst the saved ones!"*
I then awoke, joyful at what I dreamt and for the happiness gifted to the deceased man.

Where are the sighs of longing for Allah? Where are the tears of His lovers? Where is the wailing of the repentant?

By Allah, how excellent are the truthful ones, who muster the patience needed in traversing onwards till the end of life. "**Among them are those who have fulfilled their vow, and among them are those who wait, and they have not changed in the least.**"[90]

Do not consider the road of the truthful ones as difficult. For how close is the destination when the one to help you is the Helper and the one to rescue you is the Rescuer! How often has the weak one attained the goal while the avid seeker missed the mark! He is the one who does not fear poverty and He bestows abundantly. Ask from Him, who enriched the righteous, with your tongue of humbleness. May He mend your shortcomings! How splendid is the robe of one's humble brokenness before Allah.

---

90 Quran 33:23

A Lesson in Humility

Owais al-Qarni, may Allah be pleased with him, would look for food in garbage heaps when he was starving. One day, as he came to a garbage heap, he was confronted by a barking dog.
He said, *"O hound, do not harm one who does not harm you. I shall eat from my side, and you eat from yours. I am only better than you if I enter Paradise. But if I enter the Fire, then you are surely better than me."*

Alas! How much must I talk, and no one listen. Alone I speak and no one comprehends. Nothing works to help. Alas, no listener obeys.

O speaker to the seekers, where have all the seekers gone? O guider to Allah's love, where have all the lovers gone? O homes of the righteous, where are your dwellers? O rooms of the abstinent ones, where are your occupants?

My Lord, have mercy upon he who has no good deeds as an intercessor. Be kind to the one with nothing to prevent from Your wrath. Have compassion upon one who expects only goodness from You, and so clings to hope. My Lord, if You reject the sinner from Your door, where does he have left to turn? Forgive the captive to sin, O One of Beautiful Acts, by Your Mercy, O Most Merciful of those that show mercy.

Part Eight

The praise belongs to Allah, who tethered the rope of His decree, and tightened it with His power. He inscribed upon the Preserved Tablet (*al-Lawh al-Mahfouz*) every big and small thing, ensuring it is recorded therein. He "**revealed to each heaven its command**"[91] however He willed and perfected their administration. The Pen was for writing, the Tablet to be written on, and the angels for fulfilling whatever He willed and ordained. He fused ethereal spirit and material body in precise measure according to His wisdom. He made souls comprehend "**Am I not your Nurturing Lord?**" through ways hidden from their comprehension. He was not troubled in the least when He took hold of the two handfuls and said, *"These are for Paradise…and these for the Fire!"*[92]

There is no one to object to Him, no one to prevent Him or command Him. He brings near, He distances, He makes miserable, He delights, He gives glad tidings, and He warns. He distributed sustenance with the scale of His bounty, and lifespans with the scale of His justice. To where can those in His grasp flee? He enumerated all deeds in a book that "**leaves out nothing, small or great,**"[93] regardless of whether they were held in secret or openly proclaimed. He will judge them even by what is concealed in their chests with a scale so delicate, it is swayed even by an atom's weight. He will assemble

---

91 Quran 41:12

92 "Allah took hold of a handful and said, 'These are for Paradise by my Mercy.' Then He took a hold of a handful and said, 'These are for the Fire and it does not trouble Me.' – Hadith 1784, Sahih al-Jami, Albani.

93 Quran 18:49

them all upon a bridge (*al-sirat*), sharper than a sword, thinner than a strand of hair. But before that, their souls are returned to them in their graves to answer *Munkar* and *Nakir*.[94]

Glorified be He, none knows the unseen besides Him, grand and tremendous in His Majesty. I praise Him, albeit being a slave that committed what He forbade and fell short in what He commanded. I testify that there is no deity except Allah, Alone, no partner has He – a testimony that I rely on to be absolved for sins, past and future. I testify that Muhammad is His slave and messenger, who warned and cautioned of His threat and gave glad tidings of His promise. The praised Messenger, who rolled up his sleeves and dedicated his life, may the peace and blessings of Allah be upon him, his family, and his companions. They are those whom Allah purified from impurities of the heart.

O deep sleeper in the dark night of heedlessness. The first light of the convoy of death has begun to appear. By Allah, this is one departure you will not be late to miss! Yet I see the steed of your willpower standing still. I wonder, has the camel driver fallen asleep or slackened? Or is it you who has strayed from the path?

I implore you by Allah, recall the days of comfort to be enjoyed at your journey's end – "'**Peace be upon you because you were patient.' How excellent is the Final Abode!**"[95] How many precious seeds of breaths have you lost, planting them in the wastelands of wasting time?

94 The two angels responsible for questioning the deceased in their graves.

95 Quran 13:24

When will you sow them in the fertile fields of radiant deeds? Perhaps dead agarwood (*oud*) might diffuse fragrant perfume once again.

Dying Before His Death

Ibn Sammak, the preacher, narrates:

I was told about a certain worshipper so I went out to see him. I found him in a house in which he had dug his grave. He was sitting at its edge, knitting a mat out of palm leaves. I greeted him with *salaam,* and he returned my greeting softly.

"Who are you?" He asked.

"Muhammad ibn Sammak," I replied.

"The preacher?"

"Yes," I answered.

He threw the mat from his hands and said, *"O Ibn Sammak! The preacher to the listener is like the doctor to the sick. Treat me with something of your preaching."*

I said, *"O shaykh! Do you not dread that your mistakes are never forgotten? That your sins never wiped away? How many darknesses lie before you, veiling the unknown? How much horror and worry? How many punishments must be avoided? First comes the unknown darkness of the grave, then the darkness of the gathering for judgement, then the darkness of the announcement of your fate, then the darkness of the bridge (sirat), then the weighing of deeds, then the cutting off of all hopes (having no recourse to save yourself except in Allah's forgiveness), then the grasp of the King, Most High."*

He wept profusely and said, *"O Ibn Sammak, and what comes after that?"*

I said, *"The bearing of burdens and heading towards the fire. But worse than all that is the reprehension of The All-*

Compelling King."

The shaykh let out a loud cry and fell into his grave. A very old woman came and began to wipe the dirt from his face. She said, *"By my father and mother! How long did these two eyes stay awake in the obedience of Allah, Most High. How long did they cry in the fear of Allah."*
We tried to shake him awake, but it was clear he had passed away, may the mercy of Allah be upon him. I exited the house, and suddenly there was *Sari al-Saqati, Ibrahim ibn Adham, Junaid,* and a group of the righteous before me.
They asked, *"Has Abu Zaid al-Khawwas died?"*
"Yes," I replied, and directed them to his house. They entered so that they could take him out of his grave, wash him, and shroud him but found that he had already been washed, shrouded, and perfumed. The Muslims attended his funeral prayer and I returned with the group, thinking so little of myself.

A slave, long surrendered to the habit of sinning,
Found himself trapped within walls unyielding.

In despair, he sought refuge with the Merciful,
And surrendered his soul to piety, hopeful.

As night draws its curtain, his voice gasps in prayers,
Drowning in dark hours in a flood of tears.

A flame of yearning blazes within his chest,
His body scorched with sighs of grieving breaths.

Perhaps the Merciful will grace with His mercy
Upon such a sinner who dies before his death.

My Dear, for how long will you spend precious breaths in procrastination? Do you not fear to walk the path of worldly desires, so full of potholes? If you keep in mind what becomes of fat beneath the earth, it will soften your heart. Do you fatten yourself to feed your grave's worms? How much do you save so that death can spend? How much do you gather so that night and day can disperse it? How much do you beautify so that death can tarnish? How much do you relax when the reckoning will be exhaustive? How extensive are your blessings that death separates. But alas, the cries of the one on the coast do not benefit the one drowning.

Never be Complacent

One of the intimately knowledgeable ones (*arifeen*) narrates:

I saw a shaykh who would devote himself to Allah in worship and noted that his spiritual state had somewhat diminished, and he had reduced in his worship.

I asked him about that and he said, *"I committed just one error and was humiliated by it and was punished by being prevented from righteous deeds. Here I am being punished up till now..."*

My Brethren, drops of tears on cheeks blossom into everlasting legacies. Drops of clouds upon earth yield what must pass away. O assembly of sinners, seek the intercession of your tears for it is the saviour of who stands on the precipice. When the caravan of the steadfast has prepared its passengers, catch up to them in the moonlight of night prayer. By Allah, how excellent they are, whose firmness is like mighty trees, while yours is like lowly shrubs.

O delicate one of determination, when will the pawn of your repentance reach the other side of the board? Alas, the knight of heedlessness has checked the movement of your king.

Yes the taste of advice is bitter for the one who turns his back. But if the *Yousef* of your heart is impatient in the prison of worship, then even the grief of *Yaqoub* would not be enough! If you are weak in patience, then at least admit your misfortune like the brothers of *Yousef*!

My Brethren, the peace of this life did not come to the righteous till they were content and turned their hearts away from it. Their hearts were calmed by the tranquillity of humility. Their false hopes for this world were cut by the blade of serenity. It was called out to them in the marketplace of trials and tribulations, *"Will you not show patience?"* The tongues of their determination replied, *"Indeed we will!"* They were thus given the nectar of divine support to drink, sealed with musk. They forgot their selfish desires and yearned for Allah in the deserts of solitude. How many a humble, dusty one had their prayers fulfilled whenever they asked! By Allah, how excellent are "**men whom neither trade nor buying and selling distract from the remembrance of Allah.**"[96]

Real Determination

Sufyan al-Thawri, may the mercy of Allah be upon him, narrates:

96 Quran 24:37

I once saw a disabled man crawling through the desert on his way to Makkah, from the furthest non-Arab lands. He had so far spent four years on his journey. I stood looking at him in amazement with his state. He said to me, *"O Sufyan, why do you look at me?"*
"Out of wonder for the extent of your journey and the weakness of your body," I replied.
He said, *"O Sufyan, as for the distance of my journey, love has made it short. As for the weakness of my body, my Master is the one who carries it."*

O one dispelled from His door. O one barred from meeting His honoured friends. If you would like to know your value with the King, look to see what He occupies you with, and with what deeds He keeps you busy. How many come to the King's door with their tales, but He opens it only for the ones He favours. His seal is only stamped for one who comes humbly. Not every heart is worthy to be brought close. Just as not every chest harbours love. Not every wind is the soothing breeze of late night. Not everyone named *Maruf* is a *Maruf* (*al-Karkhy*). Not every *Junaid* is a *Junaid* (*al-Bagdadi*). Not every *Sari* is a *Sari* (*al-Saqati*). By Allah, how excellent are a people whose hearts brimmed with love so that the springs of their eyes flowed along the trenches of their cheeks.

My Brethren, it is as if I can sense from your hearts the sweet breeze of remorse. My Lord, whomsoever tightens the belt of repentance, do not unravel their knot of resolve. My Lord, whoever pledges to return to You, renew the acceptance of their pledge. My Lord, the wind of preaching has stirred all here, except this weak man before You, who is but joyed at the sight of the penitent. My Lord, shall they find Your forgiveness, and not I? My Lord, if I am not worthy of being forgiven, then make them intercessors for my forgiveness. Have mercy on all of us by those You have accepted from us, O Most Merciful of those who show mercy.

Part Nine

Praise belongs to Allah who guides pure hearts to unravel truths. The sincerity of the *arifeen* crystallises their hearts into jewels – a bounteous gift bestowed. The rivers of their minds burst forth with intimate knowledge (*ma'rifa*), cloaked in the robe of Allah's good-pleasure. The gardens of their familiarity with the Beloved bloom with His fragrance.

They yearn for their Beloved, the springs of their eyes dry from the pain of longing. He drove their souls to Him with the chanting of the guide of love, the fire of infatuation in their chests aflame. He watered the secrets of their hearts with the crystal waters of sincerity, their hearts' gardens flourishing with wisdom. Their inner sight is perfected with the light of *tawheed*, its rays shining forth. The guide of love drives them to Him, all the while bewildered. Still, He leads them on the path of His guardianship, they were not late, nor did they falter.

The covenant they ratified on the day of *Alast* keeps them awake with worry. They repent, respond, and remember. How many tears have flowed with the thought of His threat, their eyes like gathering clouds before the downpour. They ride on the steeds of modest sustenance and hasten along the streams of love for Allah. He seats them on thrones of His generosity, filling their chests with the gold of His remembrance. They are robed with the cloak of His good-pleasure, yet they remain in humility, barefoot and begging at His door. Their souls are delighted, their bodies radiant, their minds bejewelled, their hearts purified. Only for Allah are the sighs of the lovers and the delight of the longing ones. The skies of their eyes weep long hours in search of Him, long they stay awake.

Glorified be He who delivers the verdict of favoured or wretched in the world to come. I praise Him as one who anticipates His mercy at death, when affairs are turned upside down. I testify that there is no god except Allah, Alone, with no partner – a testimony I prepare for the Day of holding to account and when the Fire is set ablaze. I testify that Muhammad is His slave and messenger, the light of whose way outshines all others. May the peace and blessings of Allah be upon him, his family, and his companions – a prayer that I save away for a day when "**every soul will know what it has sent forth and what it has left behind.**"[97]

O gathering of penitent ones. Gather together your scattered soul through solitude, for it has been wounded by arrows of worldly desires, and cannot take flight. But if it is disciplined, then you may set it free in the skies of contemplation wherein it will catch birds of wisdoms for you. The ignorant one on the path requires a guide or will otherwise perish. As for the knowledgeable one, he has with him his equipment and preparations. If the steed of truthfulness is fattened, the mule of desires will grow weak.

Umm Da'b

Umm Da'b was a devout worshipper who had reached 90 years of age. She would perform the Hajj pilgrimage

97 Quran 82:5

every year, walking from Medina to Mecca by foot. But now she had lost her eyesight. When the time for Hajj arrived, the women visited her, crowding around her and comforting her about her lost sight. She wept and said, *"My Master, by Your Might, if I have lost the light of my sight, then I have not lost my longing for You."*

Then she entered into the state of *ihram* and began pronouncing the *labbayk* (*"Here I am, O Lord at Your service. Here I am"*).

Then she turned to her companions saying, *"There is no point to visit me again (as she would be on the pilgrimage)."* She would be walking at the forefront and sometimes outstrip the others. One of the men from her group said, *"I was amazed at her state. Then I heard a voice saying – Are you amazed at this weak one yearning for the House of her Master? He carries her to Him and guides her by the sincerity of her intention!"*

How strange! What has caused the descent of the zeal of men, whose breaths were created precious since the day the angels were commanded to prostrate to their father, until they panted like dogs feasting on the rotting world on the garbage dump of gluttony? Stones are thrown on their dusty faces, and yet they continue to return shamelessly. They depleted their drinking water watering shrubs in the desert of heedlessness. When will you redirect the water of life to the fertile land of good deeds? Perhaps it will cause dry wood to be fruitful once again.

What I Love from This World

Ibn Sammak narrates:

I was told about a certain devout worshipper living in one of the mountains of *as-Sham* (the Levant). When I had reached him, he said to me, *"O Ibn Sammak, what has made you come out to this place?"*

"I heard about you and wished to visit to you," I replied.

"The one who told you about me has deceived you. I am more knowing of my state than others." Then he continued, *"Work very hard for your salvation before your death!"*

On hearing his words, I wept, and when I decided to return home, I asked him, *"Do you have any need I can be honoured with fulfilling?"*

"Whoever sits in a place such as this has no need from where you came. Do you have any need?"

I said, *"My need is that I ask you by Allah to inform me what you love from this world and from the Hereafter."*

He wept and said, *"I would not have answered you if you had not asked me by Allah. As for what I love from this world, it is strength in doing righteous deeds while being distant from worldly desires, and a heart filled with the awe of Allah and fear of Him. As for what I love from the Hereafter, it is to hear the words from my Master, 'Go on, for I have forgiven you.'"*

He then fell to the floor, dead. I was confounded by his spiritual state. I wanted to wash him and shroud him with a part of my garments but heard a voice saying, *"Take it easy, you are not responsible for him."*

Suddenly, I could not see him. I heard water being poured over him and an alarming voice saying to him, *"Congratulations to you, O friend of Allah. You are in security from His punishment and from fear on the Day of*

Resurrection."

My Brethren, how remarkable is the burden borne by lovers on their frail frames? How much do their longing hearts endure despite their softness? How strange is their strength to bear the weight of longing? How patient are they with the fire of infatuation? Their persistence is as if made of crocodile hide. Since the sighs of lovers are smoke from the furnace of their hearts, they would be ash if not for the relief of the flow of their tears.

An Intimate Friend

One of the righteous narrates:

I once saw a man in the Sinai desert, leaning to-and-fro from weakness and emaciation. I asked him about his state, and he said, *"I am a sick man."*

"And what business does a sick man have in the desert?" I asked.

"He desires a remedy from the doctor, hoping he might find his cure. And who are you?"

I replied, *"I am a stranger to these lands."*

He said, *"O man, do you think one is ever a stranger to Allah? He is well-acquainted with one and all!"* His words caused me to weep, prompting him to ask, *"What makes you weep?"*

"An effective cure has rubbed over an infected wound," I replied.

"O man, I have pondered long over my life and contemplated deeply over my state. I found no intimate friend other than solitude. This knowledge is enough for you (to trigger change

in your life).”

My Lord, be generous on our poverty, wrought by sins, with the wealth of Your forgiveness. Be compassionate on the feebleness of our resolve with the strength of Your mercy. Soothe us from the sting of sin with the salve of repentance. Forbid us not the intercession of those You have accepted from amongst us. Have mercy on all of us all together by Your mercy, O Most Merciful of those that show mercy.

Part Ten

The praise belongs to Allah, whose perfection is far beyond comparison, similarity, or resemblance. In His Oneness, He is beyond needing a friend, or a helper, or an advisor. He is Glorified above being subjected to alteration or change. He is Supreme in His eternality, above having a companion or peer. Indeed, minds cannot grasp Him or fathom. He is matchless in His Grandeur, beyond having a father, or son, or helpers, or supporters.

He is Ultimate, beyond beginning and beyond dependence on action. Sacred in His Purity, He transcends having any limit, or being subject to change, or being confined by form, or restricted by movement, or constrained by motion. He is flawless in His Perfection, above needing thought, or requiring remembrance, or forgetting – whether it is regarding the past, present, or future. Elevated, in His Infiniteness, He transcends being bounded by an above, or a below, or a front, or a behind, a left, or a right.

He is Alone in His Eternality, above being enumerated into parts, or a whole, or being dependant on anything else, or being changed by anything else, or whatever imagination and thought deduce. In His Self-Sufficiency and His Perfection of Eternality, He is transcendent above the succession of time, days, and nights. Mighty in the honour of His Overwhelming Power, above the qualities of all, other, existent bodies, above being increased in His Perfection, above seeking to progress in His Sublimity.

By the Superiority of His Existence, he thwarts any

question of how, or dimension, or location, or measure. For all that is contradictory to the reality of He, Who exists before existence. So, it cannot be asked about when He began. Nor about how he rose above (*istiwa*) His throne. Glorified above all imperfection is He, the Elevated, the King.

No lack is found in His acts that it may be asked "if only..." Nor is the veil over His Wisdom lifted so that anyone may question "why?" Exalted is the Greatness of the Omnipotent, Majestic One. The Ever-Living, All-Powerful, All-Knowing, Efficacious of Will, Always-Hearing, Perpetually Seeing, Eloquent of Speech, Pre-existing, Ever-eternal, The Infinite, The Self-Sufficient. Glorified be He, who veils Himself with the forts of His Supremacy, rendering minds incapable of grasping the reality of His Being, leaving them confounded in words and opinions.

I praise Him, with the praise of one who stands on the shore of the sea of *tawheed*, witnessing its gravity and aware of its many dangers (of incorrect understandings). I testify that there is no deity except Allah, Alone, no partner has He – a testimony I put away for the daunting Day of horror and questioning. I testify that Muhammad is His slave and messenger, who helped us to see when we were blind, and delivered us from error. May the peace and blessings of Allah be upon him, his family, and companions – a prayer by which I anticipate his intercession, when all hopes will be cut.

My Brethren, how many promises does this world swear to fulfil, then when it delivers, it treacherously goes back on its word! No one's hopes grow at evening, except by morning they have decreased in life. This world's most truthful pledge is like that of its most treacherous inhabitant. How many of its lovers has it deceived with death, looting their lives, their wealth, and whatever their hopes had hoarded. O you who has been retired from his spiritual profession by worldly obstacles, if only you smelled the sweetness of the rose of faith, easy would you find traversing the road.

O you who finds the prison of abstinence constricting, if only you knew it was as spacious as a desert. You would be thankful instead of casting complaints. *Yousef* did not see the honour of "**Truly this day you are of high rank and trusted in our presence**"[98] except after the constriction of "**So he remained in prison for several years.**"[99]

A Wonder

A renowned reciter of the Qur'an with a beautiful voice entered into Mecca. *Ali ibn al-Fudayl* came to know about it and requested his presence. He said, *"It has reached me that you are a fine reciter, so recite for us something from the Qur'an."*

He replied, *"I fear that perhaps you will be overly-affected by hearing the Qur'an from me, and that your father might lose you, and he is from amongst the righteous."*
"I request that you fulfil my request," Ali insisted.
So he began to read until he reached "**If only you could**

98 Quran 12:54
99 Quran 12:42

see when they shall stand before the Fire, saying, 'Would that we were sent back! Then we would not deny the signs of our Lord, but we would be among the believers!'"[100] He had not completed the verse, except that Ali fell down. The people waited for him to get back up, but he did not. They shook him, only to realise that he had passed away. News of his death spread, and cries were heard. The news reached his father, and he made his way to his son in complete tranquillity, the people following him. He said, *"May the mercy of Allah be upon you, Ali. I always feared death for you when you would hear the book of Allah, Mighty and Majestic. You have gone ahead, we shall certainly catch up with you."*

Then he looked to the people and at how many of them had crowded around and said, *"It is not a wonder that Ali has died because of his fear of Hellfire. Rather it is a wonder that one is threatened with Hellfire but has no fear of Allah."*

How amazing it is! I do not know if the one to whom I speak is present or absent! How much do I urge those that have no love for the Beloved? My Brethren, I ask you by Allah, be present of heart for even a moment! You whose heart has become cold over the winter of worldly desires! Your nature is to be moved by sin, to be stagnant for acts of obedience. Do you not have a mind with which you realise the purpose of your creation? How long is the slumber of your heedlessness? To whom shall I speak? Where is the shame brought on by understanding?

---

100 Quran 6:27

The Slave's Flaw

One of the righteous narrates:

I passed by a market and heard someone selling a cheap slave while absolving himself of every flaw the slave had. I neared the slave, who was just a youth, and asked, *"What is this flaw that you have?"*

He replied, *"My master, I have many flaws. I am not sure which one he is referring to."*

So I asked the seller, *"What is the flaw of this slave?"*

"He has the sickness of madness," came his reply.

I turned to the youth and asked, *"Are you overtaken by fits? Do they occur once a week? Or is it every month?"*

"My master, I am overpowered with the malady of love in the heart. It spreads over my limbs and takes control of them. The intoxication of love makes the mind fly away with the mention of the Beloved. The body faints and remains still. The ignorant one thinks it madness."

I realised that the youth was from the *awliya* (friends) of Allah, Most High. So I asked the seller, *"How much for this boy?"*

"Two hundred silver dirhams."

I gave him an extra twenty and took the youth to my house and told him to enter. He refused, saying, *"My master, do you not have a family?"*

"Yes."

"And who is permitted to look at unrelated (non-mahram) women?"

"I allow you to enter," I said.

"God forbid! Do you not have a need I can fulfil from outside the door?"

I remained silent and left him there as I entered the house. I returned with some food for him, but he said, *"I am fasting."*

When night fell, he stood up to pray in the corridor of the house, and I brought him a container of water so he could refresh his ablution. I came to see him again in the middle of the night and found him standing in prayer. He did not notice me as he wept and said, *"My Lord, the kings have locked their doors, and Your door is open. My Lord, eyes have fallen asleep, thoughts have finally subsided, and every beloved is alone with their beloved. My Lord, be generous with Your Forbearance upon the one who desires nothing but You. My Lord, if You reject me from Your door, then to whose door can I seek refuge?"*

Then he made a long prostration and said, *"The arifeen have made their worship sincere for You. By Your Generosity, the righteous have been guided. O Excellent One in forgiving, let me savour Your forgiveness and the sweetness of Your mercy."* He continued like that until he prayed the *fajr* prayer.
In the morning, I approached him and asked, *"How did you sleep last night?"*
"My master, does one sleep when he fears the Fire and knows at night his deeds are presented to the King, the Compeller? Remembrance of the Fire has prevented me from sleep." Then he wept for a while.
I said to him, *"Go, for I free you for the sake of Allah."*
He wept some more and said, *"My master, I used to have my rewards multiplied twice. The reward of worshipping Allah and the reward of serving my earthly master. One of those rewards has now ended."*

I handed him some money, but he refused to accept it, saying, *"Indeed, the Guarantor of sustenance is alive."*

I urged him to take it, but he refused to take anything from it. He finally left, walking as if unsure where to go.

O one whose heart is counterfeit! How will you fare when the examiner of authenticity is Allah? Where is the joy when hearing His remembrance? Where is the yearning for Him in this exile?

How many companions have passed on the road, "**whose sides shun (their) beds, calling upon their Nurturing Lord out of fear and hope,**"[101] and you were not amongst them? How many a night-traveller joined the caravan of "**little of the night did they slumber,**"[102] yet you were not with them? How many have had their stories of repentance with the Mighty One written, yet you have no story. O slumbering one in the night of heedlessness, the caravan has set out and you have not moved! The companions have departed but you have not noticed.

An Extremely Busy Youth

One of the righteous narrates:
I was travelling over one of the mountains of *al-Sham* when I suddenly heard a weak voice saying, *"If only my heart be sincere in my worry and complaint! For the calamity has magnified, and the trial has become great!"*
I followed the voice until I found a young man sitting in a prayer niche weeping. When he stopped, I greeted him and said, *"My dear, what makes you cry in this state?"*

101 Quran 32:16
102 Quran 51:17

"And how can I not cry when I have been removed from His door and prevented from complaining to Him."
"My dear, I would like to ask you something. May I?"
"Ask away uncle but make it quick. For I have worries to be concerned with. I have much to do, and before me are great obstacles to be traversed and horrors to be witnessed. All the while, night and day hasten to seek my death."
I asked, *"What is it that makes it binding upon Allah to bring His friends close to Him?"*

Upon hearing that he fell unconscious. When he was revived he said, *"By their dismissing everything besides Allah. By their taking only what is necessary from this world to fulfil their obligations. By abandoning unnecessary speech. By solitude."*

Then he left me alone and moved on.

How strange that sleep ties people back from reaching the great ones! The signal of departure goes unnoticed as the caravan embarks, and the pleasant chant of the guide propels them forward at a swift pace.

My Brethren, only one of fine spiritual taste can savour the honey of my words. Such words do not move except one of longing. This gathering is a robe, its embroidery is its preaching. The hand of divine care robes those that shiver with repentance. The fragrant breeze of yearning wafts over pure hearts.

My Lord, speech unaided by Your blessing bears no

fruit. My Lord, the attendees of this gathering have endeavoured to knock at Your door. Each one of them has a story, and they have elevated their plight to You. They have draped themselves with a shawl of shame, either out of shyness to You, or due to their belittling themselves, or out of fear of their previous sins.

My Lord, dispatch the envoys of Your forgiveness and command them to receive the stories in their hands. My Lord, every story has written within it "**we and our family have been touched with hardship.**"[103] Each story is sealed with "**If You do not forgive us and have Mercy upon us, we shall surely be among the losers.**"[104] My Lord, stamp just once upon our stories "**There is no blame on you today. May Allah forgive you.**"[105] My Lord, forgive our sins. Do not let us return from Your door empty-handed, O Most Merciful of those that show mercy.

103 Quran 12:88
104 Quran 7:23
105 Quran 12:92

Part Eleven

The praise belongs to Allah, who opened the doors of success and spiritual kindnesses for His sincere slaves. He inundates all His creation with abundant gifts unasked. He calls out from the podium of the furthest point of night – My slaves! Is there anyone ill? Is there anyone seeking forgiveness? Is there anyone to ask from Me? He made misfortunes as signposts leading to His *tawheed* and to praising Him with increased appreciation – how effective those signposts are.

He made this world a dwelling, its years serving as waypoints, its days a measure of our progress. He created its grief, a darkness whose shadow passes away and its joy, a spark whose brightness is but fleeting. Indeed, its amusement is spoiled with sorrow just as health is shadowed by sickness. The days spent here are a measly few. What is allowed in it (*halal*) entails being called into account while what is forbidden (*haram*) incurs punishment. As for the consequences of deeds, some are reimbursed here, others are delayed till the Hereafter. Its light adjoins to its dark. The sweetness of its lusts is wrapped in sin and its shine is a facade, an imitation. The jewels of its beauty are only borrowed and await repayment. The purity of its life is tarnished with troubles. All who seek it return empty-handed. The conclusion of its gatherings is separation. The full moon of its perfection is for it to wane and disappear. The stars of its glitter undoubtedly fade.

The *arifeen* see it for what it is, and so lower the sights of their hearts from it. They know its promises are false, and so they removed themselves from its preoccupations and desires, its people and places, its tribe, and its clan. They see no power in material causes and means. They distanced themselves too from brethren and beloved, preparing for a death that is already on its way.

The one awake to this world is asleep, while the one asleep to it is awake. The intelligent one does not let his hopes become entangled in its web. The fat of it is bony, its pleasures are poison, and the one who stretches his hand out to it is shackled.

So Glorified be He, above all imperfection, who tests His creation by its allurement, leaving none of us immune. I praise Him with the praise of one who anticipates His mercy in the present and His forgiveness in the future. I testify that there is no god except Allah, Alone, no partner has He. He is the refuge of every terrified one and the hope of every hopeful one. I testify that Muhammad is His slave and messenger who was honoured with receiving His messenger-ship, and cherished by his name included in prayers, a means for every supplicator. May the peace and blessings of Allah be upon him, his family, and companions – a prayer that I keep, for a momentous and terrible day.

O one ensnared by his lusts, you have lost your way. O one who blunts the blade of his resolve in seeking this world, you have missed the mark. O feeble of fortitude, ponder on the toil and pains of Adam, on the weeping and resoluteness of *Nuh*. *Ibrahim*, the Friend of Allah, was subjected to fire. *Yacoub* lost his sight with his weeping throughout the night. *Yousef* was tested as a prisoner and a slave. *Zachariah* was sawn apart with a saw. *Ayyub* was tested with misfortune after misfortune. *Dawud* wept till plants grew where his tears planted. *Sulaiman's* reign was troubled even as king. *Musa* was reduced to tending goats after being exiled from his home. Jesus, son of *Maryam,* roamed the dry and lonely desert. And Muhammad, peace and blessings be upon him and all the Prophets, embraced a life of poverty.

Do you then seek success with just empty wishes? How misguided that is! But an unworthy man may wear the garment of the lovers of Allah, and perhaps a man will accompany one who does not suit him.

A Conversation with the Earth

Once the Prophet Jesus, upon him be peace, passed by a village, whose inhabitants had all perished. Jesus, upon him be peace, called out, *"O land, where are your people?"*

Allah, Most High, commanded the earth to reply to him, so it said, *"O soul from Allah, their deaths have prevented them from their homes. Their hopes for attaining this world deceived them. Their wealth misled them about their imminent deaths. They were surrounded by their misdeeds, and their sins became shackles over their necks. Their spirits were presented before the King, the Creator. Their lives were temporary, their bones disintegrated. Do you see any trace of them left? They are to be called to account over their past days, and the angels of Hell will be their escort. Then either towards lofty gardens, or a scorching fire."*

Jesus, upon him be peace, wept profusely as did his companions. He turned to them and said, *"This is the conclusion of this world. So woe to the one who prefers it over service to the Master."*

My Brethren, only those whom the King personally oversees can enter His majestic presence. Each heart is turned towards the objective it strives for. How many steps, once misplaced, did the divine Will realign. It lured the one dormant and spurred them to action. The life of *Umar* was marked by folly till he heard the divine call in the bazaar of love calling out "so flee to Allah." That favoured one, slumbering on the bed of heedlessness, paid attention saying, "Who will witness my trade and take the price of my soul?" It was said the witness waits for your coming at the house of *Arqam*, a coming decreed since before time.

This chain of events was stirred by the prayer, *"Dear Lord, strengthen this religion by the more beloved man to You from these two – Abu Jahl or Umar ibn al-Khattab"*[106] on the tongue of the beloved Prophet, the peace and blessings of Allah be upon him. He entered the house, may Allah be pleased with him, dressed for war, but when the glance of the loving one fell on the beloved *Umar*, love overflowed with the recognition of prophethood. The attraction of that merciful one pulled him in, the way of success opened before him, and he swore that "Allah would not be worshipped in secret after this day while *Umar* is alive!"

My Brethren, I speak of the exalted realms of Paradise, but

106 Hadith 3681, Jami al-Tirmidhi

you are content with the empty chests of heedlessness. How many simple stories of the righteous have I sung, but you have not moved to their rhythm. A longing heart travels far even while one has not moved. How fast does one excel when he makes a little effort!

O *Bilal*! How splendid are you that the steed of divine care carried you to the divine Prescence, yet *Abu Talib* could not arrive at the destination. O *Ibn Adham*! How excellent are you that gatherings of remembrance are fragranced with your memory. O *Rabiah (al-Adawiyah)*! How excellent are you in your response to His call, occupying a throne of lofty eminence. O *Salman (al-Farsi)*! Upon which steed did you arrive from Persia till divine care included you in *"Salman is from us, the family of the Prophet."*[107]

He Selects for His Mercy Who He Wills

It has been mentioned that a worshipper remained in a cave in Egypt for forty years. One day as he was sitting, a youth appeared with some food and water to also seclude himself alone. He ate and drank as the worshipper began to recite "**Has not the time come for those who believe for their hearts to be humbled to the remembrance of Allah...**"[108] The youth looked left and right and didn't see anyone else around (and thought he was being addressed). He returned to his cup to drink, and the worshipper repeated the verse.

This time, the youth threw the cup from his hand and said, *"Certainly, by Allah, the time has arrived!"*

107 Hadith 6600, Mustadarak al-Hakim.

108 Quran 57:16

He got down from his place, not knowing where to go, weeping, and all the while saying, "*Certainly, by Allah, the time has arrived…by Allah!*"

The worshipper followed him and saw that before the youth was a body of water blocking his way. But the youth placed his foot on the water and began walking upon it. He looked back at the worshipper saying, "*Certainly, by Allah, the time has arrived…the time has arrived!*"

The worshipper too placed his foot on the water, but it sank immediately. He said, "*My Lord, what is wrong with me? I have been knocking at Your door for forty years and I have not reached what this one attained in a single moment!*"

He suddenly heard a voice saying, "**He selects for His Mercy whomsoever He wills…**"[109]
He was overcome with tears and returned to his cave, in a broken and humbled state.

My Brethren, when the authority of divine decree assigns one with the governorship of His friendship, the banners of divine care are hoisted high for them. As for the deprived, they have no means.

When the breeze of divine support blows before dawn, divine care moves the branches that are the hearts of those seeking forgiveness. The leaves that are their tongues rustle with all varieties of prayers and supplications.

109 Quran 3:74

My Lord, release our captives from the shackles of sin. Have mercy on the humble ones before You. O Remover of the harm that touched *Ayyub*, draw us to You with the guiding reins of divine care. Do not cast us away from Your door. Do not sever our hands of hope from the rope of Your forgiveness. O Most Merciful of those who show mercy! And send prayers and blessings upon our master, Muhammad, his family, and companions.

Part Twelve

The praise belongs to Allah who delighted, by bringing them close, a people who were truthful to Him in their thoughts and depths of their hearts. He especially blessed them, since before time, so wayward thoughts would lose their way with them. He lit, with the lamps of their hearts, the roads towards intimate knowledge of Him (*ma'rifa*). Thus, the darkness of their minds was illuminated with radiant realities. He taught their minds the topic of *tawheed* in the primary school of the day of *Alast*. They copied the lesson on the preserved tablets of their outer and inner forms. They were honoured with the sweet robe of intimate prayer and supplication, and the garden of their sincerity was fragrant with their acceptance into His circle.

Their chests are filled and overflowing with wisdom's water. The bird-song of their worship provokes a reminiscence of their return to Him, so they are entranced by the remembrance of Him, the Hidden One, the Present One. Around them swirl drinks of divine care, spilling with the anguish of separation from Him, and they grasp the jugs in the late hours of night. The night of secluded prayer is stretched over them with the pegs of darkness, and they complain of their longing in the depth of night and the sweltering day. When the veils fall, they contemplate their Master, without barrier or obstacle. Such are the spiritual states of the blessed ones! As for the wretched, who will heed their complaints of misery?

For Allah, the *arifeen* dedicate the profits of their time.

Divine support adorns them, and with their mention, gatherings and pulpits are adorned. Their recollection embroiders distant horizons and nearby pages through what inkwells dictate and notepads recount of their virtues.

Glorified be He, who gave them success in His service, and preserved them from small slips and major transgressions. He abandoned the wretched to wander the desert of heedlessness, lost and disoriented by their crimes. I praise Him with the praise of one who recognises His overflowing blessings and is grateful, fully aware of being undeserving. I testify that there is no god except Allah, Alone, no partner has He – a testimony that I keep for the day of death and horror of the grave.

I testify that Muhammad is His slave and messenger. Who assailed with his sword the evil blasphemer and obstinate denier. May the prayers and blessings of Allah be upon him, his family, and companions, every moment the palms of leaves applaud and birds sing from their branches.

My Brethren, the night is the mount for those that pray *tahajjud* (late night prayer). Recital of the Quran is their chanting guide. At the approach of dawn, the flags of honoured stations are hoisted. By dawn all their goods for sale are brought and lined up. On the Day when the bazar of the Hereafter opens, they shall receive the profit of "**No soul knows what comfort is kept hidden for it as a recompense for that which they used to do.**"[110] On that day, the sleeping one will bite their fingers in regret.

---

110 Quran 32:17

What You've Heard is Enough for You

One of the *arifeen* narrates:

I saw *Banan al-Hammal* after his death in my dream and asked him, *"What has Allah done with you?"*

"He forgave me," he replied.

"Through which deed?" I inquired.

"Through my patience in His service and my shyness before His Honour."

"And where is your home?"

"In Jannat al-Firdaus (the highest Paradise)."

"Through which deed did you achieve that?"

"Through my haste in performing deeds in obedience to Him and my abandonment of His disobedience."

"And through which deed do the friends of Allah deserve to be given a spiritual state in which they fear Allah?"

He recited, "**Whomsoever Allah guides, he is rightly guided.**"[111]

Then I asked, *"What is the way to gain success?"*

"Restrain your tongue and be conscious of Allah wherever you are, you will find Him before you." Then he said, *"What you have heard is enough for you."*

By Allah, how excellent were they, those "**who have been true to that which they pledged unto Allah,**"[112] "**whom neither trade nor buying and selling distract from the remembrance of Allah.**"[113] The feet of their worship are as firm as mountains, while those of the heedless are on a loose precipice. The chanting guide of their love impels

111 Quran 17:97
112 Quran 33:23
113 Quran 24:37

them forward amidst the caravan of hearts until they reach a station of truthfulness.

My Brethren, whoever is lost in the darkness of their oppression is destroyed. The aspirer of worldly desires seeks death with his own hand. O killer of themselves with a noose of sin, how terribly misguided are your choices. Time and again, has the emergence of white hair served as a warning, but you paid no heed, nor were you moved to action. Instead, you dyed them with the darkness of heedlessness. If your life is turning away from you, and death is hastening forward, how quickly will they meet!

Old Wood is Used for Fire

Salih al-Marri narrates:
One day a slave girl, known for her singing, passed by a Qur'an reciter as he recited "**And verily, Hell is the promised abode for them all.**" She let out a shriek and fell unconscious. When she was revived, she broke her musical instruments. She began to dedicate herself to worship, exerting herself intensely in its path until she became renowned for it. I visited her once and talked to her about taking it easy on herself. She wept and said, *"Oh, if only I knew the state of those in their graves – how will they exit from them, and if only I knew how they will cross over the bridge (sirat), and how will they free themselves from the horrors of the Day of Judgement, and how will they hear the rebuke of their Master!"* Then she lost consciousness.
When she came around, she said, *"My Master and Owner, when I was youthful and green, I disobeyed You. It is only now, being old and dry wood, that I obey You."* Then she turned to

me, saying, *"Don't you see it is dry wood that is used for fire! How many a disgrace will be uncovered on that Day!"*

O one drowning in the sea of heedlessness. The lovers of Allah have journeyed with the caravan of patience, traversing the land of longing for Him, settling in the garden of His intimacy. Their breaths were perfumed with the fragrance of His closeness, the breeze of having arrived at the goal wafted over them. But one slain by heedlessness remains oblivious. None hears our talk, except one of hearing. None understands its meanings except one with a heart. None is present in our gatherings except one with spirit.

My Brethren, how swiftly is the heart filled with empty hopes undone! One has dreams to build buildings of bricks, but perhaps the bricks of his grave have already been forged. You speak to yourself of profits imported from afar, but perhaps your corpse's shroud has already arrived at a nearby store. Know that knowledge is gold and action is silver, and one must be exchanged for the other. O one who has not shown up at Allah's door, who has been absent when white hair has been present, and has not repented, hurry. Hasten, before the opportunity is lost, and the door bolted shut.

Leave them be.

When *Utbah,* the youth, repented in the gathering of *Abdul Wahid ibn Zayd,* he wept till he lost consciousness. A few men came to *Abdul Wahid* and said, *"O shaykh. This youth is weeping too much, tell him to go easy on himself."*

He responded to them, *"Shall Utbah weep over his past sins and I prevent him? It would then be said to me – you did not weep, and yet you prevented others from weeping? You were not pained with regret, yet you prevented the one who is burning? You did not wail, but you prevented the one who wailed?"*

How strange, that I flash my warning signs upon your heart, yet still you speed down the roads of heedlessness. It appears as if an infection spreads over your eye, one the doctor's remedy cannot heal. When the light of prophethood shined, unveiling horizons of guidance, *Salman the Persian* saw it, but the neighbourly *Abu Talib* did not.

When the lamp of messenger-ship was set alight in the night of disbelief, *Umar* came forth, aspiring towards the Messenger, meeting him in the house of *Arqam*. The hand of the seeker rapped on the door of repentance. It was called out that the arrow of *"one of the two men"*[114] has struck its mark! For if divine care looks down on one, then the rivers of preaching will flow onto the gardens of his heart, and springs of virtuous deeds burst into bloom. But the sign of Allah's anger is being struck with the drought of humility and barrenness of fear.

---

114 That is the prayer of the Prophet, that was mentioned earlier – "Dear Lord, strengthen this religion by the more beloved man to You from these two – Abu Jahl or Umar ibn al-Khattab".

One does not holiday by the river Tigris except those who can afford it. One does not rest from the fatigue of the journey until they arrive home. And how severe is the distress of the one who misses his flight and is separated from his companions?

How strange is my affliction? I remind others yet I am heedless myself. My Master, how severe is my calamity, that I try to awake others, yet I am sleeping myself. My Master, my situation is dire, that I endeavour to guide others, but am lost myself. My Lord, be mercifully generous upon this pretender, who concludes his advice and preaching here, but it did not occur to his mind to remedy and treat his own self. My Lord, if You guide Your seekers through my preaching, do You see it fitting to accept the listener but reject the speaker? My Lord, if my words are not sincere for Your sake in this gathering, then make whomsoever is sincere a reason to overlook my shortcomings, by Your Light! Have mercy upon all of us, O Most Merciful of those that show mercy.

Part Thirteen

The praise belongs to Allah, who established the order of the universe upon the pillar of His Power, without partner, or helper. He originated ethereal spirits in the unseen realm, "**Blessed is Allah, the best of creators.**"[115] He is the One who contrived dense bodies, "**And indeed, We created man from an essence of clay.**"[116] He joined soul with body through a mystery that eludes the grasp of minds. He bound the monster that is the mind with the rope of reason, before imprisoning it within the bounds of the laws of His creation. He arranged the scale of deeds upon the balance of His Omnipotence, so this deed is placed on the right pan, and that, on the left.

He raised the tent of the heavens upon the pillars of His Absolute Dominance, then beautified it with celestial lights. Then "**made them missiles against the devils.**"[117] He made the wellsprings of clouds to weep with the teardrops of rain, coaxing gardens to burst into blossoms of laughter. The chanting guide of thunder leads the caravan of clouds, so they carry their loads of sustenance to those in need. With the soul of rain, the corpse of earth is given life. Plants are resurrected from their earthly tombs, a lesson for all onlookers. All of that shows the resurrection of humankind before the Lord of all that exists. All the world is under the command of His will, from the first to the last.

He prepared death for His creation and hamstrung them with His decree. But the *arifeen* are content with whatever

115 Quran 23:14
116 Quran 23:12
117 Quran 67:5

He wills.

Glorified be the One in Whose grasp is taking and giving – for those in the heavens and earth. I praise Him with the praise of one whose shortcomings have barred him from attaining the stations of the righteous. I testify that there is no god except Allah, Alone, no partner has He – a testimony I nurture as a conviction till the Day of Resurrection. I testify that Muhammad is His slave and messenger, the elect of the prophets, master of the messengers, may the prayers and blessings of Allah be upon him, his family, and companions – the cream of the crop.

My Brethren, for whoever the stamp of Allah's closeness appears, the guide to a blissful end takes their hand along the path. The trees of guidance are planted within their hearts, irrigated with waters of Divine protection. Indeed, the fruits of intimate knowledge (*ma'rifa*) are upon the branches of their tongues, with fruits close at hand to hearts close to Allah. Such is Allah's favour upon whom He wills, but none blames His decree for their failings except one with a sickness.

Umair ibn Wahb

When Umair ibn Wahb, may Allah be pleased with him, reached Medina, he tied up his mount, and entered into the presence of the Chosen One, may the peace and blessings of Allah be upon him. He carried his sword upon his shoulder. When Umar, may Allah be pleased with him, saw him, he said, *"O Messenger of Allah, be careful of this treacherous one."*

The Chosen One, may the peace and blessings of Allah be upon him, said, *"What has brought you here, O Umair?"*
"To pay the ransom for some prisoners with you."[118]
"And why is there a sword hanging from your shoulder?"
"May Allah curse such swords, which did not benefit us!"
Then the Chosen One, may the prayers and blessings of Allah be upon him, said, *"O Umair, did you and Safwan not sit at the Hajr (spot by the Ka'ba), remembering the people of al-Qaleeb*[119] *from amongst Quraish? You both said that there was no goodness in life after their deaths. Then you said to him that if not for your dependants and debts, you would head out to Muhammad and relieve your pain by killing him. Then Safwan guaranteed to pay your debt and look after your family (if you did so). Thus, you came here to kill me. But Allah, Most High, is between me and you."*
Umair glorified Allah and said, *"I testify that there is no god except Allah, and you, Muhammad, are the Messenger of Allah! By Allah, O Messenger of Allah, that happened between us and there was no third with us, except the One who informed you of it. And no one else came to know of it. So praise be to Allah, who brought me here for my guidance!"*
The Messenger of Allah smiled, may the peace and blessings of Allah be upon him, and said, *"Teach your (new) brother his religion, and hasten to release his captives."*

My Brethren, the one who remains uncertain of his fate after death is not deluded by the empty hopes of

118 This was after the Battle of Badr.
119 A well in which the corpses of the polytheists of the Quraysh tribe were thrown into in the aftermath of the Battle of Badr. It included their leaders, who were most obstinate in their animosity to the Muslims.

his imagination. Just as a dreamer, who bothers not to interpret them, is not deluded by dreams. When blissful bodies enter the orbit of the sun of His acceptance, the ripe hearts of those penitent ones are illuminated with the light of their Nurturing Lord.

Under the cover of night, the soldiers of sleep and the soldiers of prayer line up for battle. Leading the army of prayer is the advance guard of "**who recite Allah's verses throughout the night, prostrating.**"[120] Leading the army of sleep is the vanguard of "**Had Allah known of any good in them, He would have certainly caused them to hear.**"[121] With the appearance of the banner of dawn, the army of laziness and sleep is decisively defeated. The sun hardly rises but the spoils have already been distributed. You took no part of the booty since you took no part in the battle.

A Sincere Repentance

One of the righteous narrates:

I had an old woman as a neighbour, whose son was excessive in sin. After a while, he got sick. When death approached, he regretted his past misdeeds and awoke from his heedlessness. He said to his mother, *"If I die, then do not inform anyone of my death. For I know they will not pray over me. And just make my grave here in my house. I know that I harmed my neighbours throughout my life, and I would not like to bother my neighbours of my grave after my death."*

---

120 Quran 3:113
121 Quran 8:23

After he had passed away, his mother did what he asked and buried him in his house. She wept over him saying, *"My son, how great is your loneliness! How severe is your trial! You have become a prisoner in your grave and our reunion is not until the Day of Judgement."* Then she stood awhile, asking Allah, Glorified and Majestic, to see him in her dream.

After some time, she saw him in her sleep while he was in an elegant garden, amongst brilliant lights, and on his forehead it was written with light: *"Such is the state of a slave who recognised his humility and regret over his sins. Who was ashamed over what he committed and perpetrated. His Master has forgiven him."*

His mother asked him, *"My son! Tell me about your affair, what happened?"*

He replied, *"When I was taken, my Master made me stand before Him and He said – O My slave, do they not know that I am your Master, so why would they abandon you and not pray over you, narrowing the road of mercy before you, as if My forgiveness for your sins is constricted? Then you feared to be buried near others so as not to harm them. By My Glory and Majesty. I have forgiven everyone buried near you as a gift for your shame and a mercy for your poverty and humility before Me."*

My Brethren, the desert of night is crossed on a light, swift camel at the head of the caravan, while the heavy are burdened down with loads at the rear. By Allah, how excellent are the people of night, walking on the feet of *tahajjud* (night prayer), rolling up the distances of night, until they reach the destination. By morning, they praise Allah for the distance they traversed towards Him. Such zeal aspires to the peak of the loftiest mountain. The motivation of the one who falls short is the lusts of his stomach and genitals.

The Doctor's Cure

One of the righteous, when asked about the conditions around his repentance, said:

I pondered one day about my sins, my shortcomings, and my final judgement. I found my life decreasing, my sins increasing, my final judgement approaching, and my self (*nafs*) not agreeing to turn in repentance. This was a calamity even mountains could not bear.

I left my house, pondering at my terrible state of affairs. I came across a doctor who was surrounded by patients, seeking their medicines. I stood amongst them and said to the doctor, *"O shaykh, do you have any cure for sins?"*

He pondered a moment, then raised his head, and said, *"If the sinner knows against Whom he sins, he would melt before he sins."*

I returned home and found that his words had an effect on my heart. So I clung to the door of my Master until He accepted me.

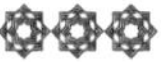

If only I knew, when you, O poor one, would turn to repentance. When will your heart yearn to be amongst the cherished ones?

My Dear, whoever takes his place amongst the soldiers

of strenuous effort, will find their spoils multiplied. Whoever fills the dwelling of their time with *dhikr* (remembrance of Allah), his profits will be accumulated on the Day of need. Whoever fervently strives for His contentment, endures the heat of being turned upon the coals of relentless trials until they arrive at their desired destination.

The first station on the path is the exertion of the heart. Second, a step in the exertion of body and wealth. Third, a step towards the station of sincerity. This is the road of the seekers, where are the travellers? These are the stations, where are those to disembark? These are subtle points of truth, where are those who can discern them? These are melodies of wisdom, who will lend an ear? These are depths of meanings, who will seek to understand?

My Dear, you work for this world and have yet to attain it. How do you plan to attain the Hereafter without working for it? And if you are lazy in seeking this world, how will you seek the Hereafter? If you are weak in the face of the bodily desires, how will you reach the deeds of the upright ones? The house of your heart has been emptied of the inhabitants of love for Him, but no one is weeping.

My Lord, the purpose of the doctor's toil is to know the cause and prescribe the cure, and good health depends upon Your command. My Lord, our malady is sin, while the cure is repentance and Your acceptance of us.

My Lord, how often a strong one was devoured by the desert, while the weak arrived at the destination.

My Lord, how many a seeker did You turn away from and so they were ruined. How many a sinner did You mercifully gaze upon, so they were awakened. My Lord, bestow upon us a repentance that binds us to You, O Most Merciful of those who show mercy.

Part Fourteen

The praise belongs to Allah who crowned the *arifeen* with the crown of His friendship, drawing near what is distant. He made their spirits declare His oneness on the day of *Alast*. He made the minds of their inner sight contemplate the characteristics of His Oneness. He is far supreme above being confined to a body or being limited.

The *arifeen* recognise the signs of His Oneness by the signposts of His creations, they deny polytheism in all its forms, and reject the notion of Him having offspring. The dawn of delight rises over sights of their hearts, from the horizons of righteous deeds, bathing them in blissful morning light.

He caused rivers of wisdom to flow down the waterways of their tongues, and their water continues to collect. He nurtures the pearls of *dhikr* in the shells of their hearts, and waters them with their tears. Glorifications, praises, and exaltations crystallise in result.

Such hearts are surrounded by the trees of lengthy prayers, their canopy stretching far, shades them. Its gardens are tended to by streams of contemplation, the handiwork of One who originates creation and repeats it.

The lonely seeker is drawn to the fragrance of the *arifeen*. Around them swirl stirring drinks in cups of love, amongst them is the one visibly affected and amongst them is the stoic, showing restraint. The resonance of their supplication reverbs in melodies, with pitches high and low.

Glorified be the One Who divided creation into two – the fortunate ones, and the wretched. I praise Him with the praise of one who was humbled by life and so he exchanged what he willed for what the Willing One willed. I testify that there is no god except Allah, Alone, no partner has He – a testimony I store away for the Day eyes will widen in horror. I testify that Muhammad is His slave and messenger. Who, through his way, bound every obstinate devil, and was followed by those destined for delight, in this world and the next. May the peace and blessings of Allah be upon him, his family, and companions – a prayer I prepare for the Day it will be said to Hell, "**'Have you been filled?' And it will reply, 'Is there any more?'**"[122]

My Brethren, how often is the crop harvested too soon?[123] The one who realises the significance of years is not deceived by the trickery of good health. How could the one who has reached sixty deny the dread his state demands? How does the one who reaches seventy not eye his residence of death? How does the one of fourty not sense their decline?

Haram (forbidden) consumed is fuel, stored in the body, for a fire. When the furnace of death begins, it is set alight, and all opportunities are burnt to dust. The eating of *haram* is a gluttonous dog consuming a carcass. The *haram* is a poisoned arrow, spreading through the soul, rotting the heart, congealing tears of the eye, inducing deafness upon the ears, rendering the mind dumb, the

122 Quran 50:30

123 i.e., How often does one die in their youth.

tongue mute of *dhikr*, binding their feet from taking a step in His path. Alas, the madman does not realise whether he is dead or alive.

For the Likes of Such

Muhammad ibn al-Munkadir had a servant boy working for him (in his clothing store) where they would write the price of garments upon each item. One day, the boy sold a robe, on which it was written five dirhams, to a (probably illiterate) bedouin for ten. When *Ibn al-Munkadir* arrived, the boy informed him about the bedouin, thinking it would please his master. Instead, *Ibn al-Munkadir* said, *"How badly you have done."*

Ibn al-Munkadir went out in search of the bedouin until he caught up with him and said, *"The boy made a mistake, he charged you an extra five dirhams."*
The bedouin replied, *"Its fine, I am happy with the sale."*
"If you are content with it, then I am not content with it for you. If you like, I can return you five dirhams, or give you another garment."

The bedouin agreed to receive the five dirhams and *Ibn al-Munkadir* left. It was said to the bedouin that the man was *Muhammad ibn al-Munkadir*. The bedouin glorified Allah and said, *"By Allah, for the likes of such does Allah send down rain when we are hit with drought."*

Alas, how we long to see a household of men like those amongst our houses. But neighbourhoods have emptied, devoid of inhabitants of that calibre.

My Dear, every garment can be washed, except that of the phoenix, its washing is fire. I fear the garment of your deeds resembles it. Do you not see those drowning in their worldly desires as those described with "**Their commerce has not brought them profit, and they are not rightly guided.**"[124]

The *haram* is like a matchstick for the firewood of one's soul, it but awaits the striking of judgement. For now, the heedless do not perceive the danger but "**...you will certainly know its truth before long.**"[125] How gleeful are they on the mat of empty hopes even though "**these have not received a tenth of what We had granted those (their predecessors).**"[126] Even if you are given a moment's reprieve, your time may come at any moment. By Allah, how excellent are those who patiently persevere to the diet of abstinence, their burdens lightened.

O miserable one, your four sides are surrounded by four dangers leading to ruin: old age, prevention from righteousness, indulgence in sins, and the onslaught of misfortunes. When the garment is filthy, the body dirty, and the heart impure, where are the cleansing tears of contemplation? Where is the purifying regret of bygone days? What have we learnt from the tears of those we grieved? Little did they think they would be separated, "**Do you perceive even one of them, or hear from them a murmur?**"[127]

---

124 Quran 2:16
125 Quran 38:88
126 Quran 34:45
127 Quran 19:98

My Dear, if the robe of your rewards is punctured with the thorns of disobedience, then mend it with a thread of remorse. Only the one lost for a few days hopes to find the road again. The one lost for fifty years may very well have perished.

O you who but aims for the city's walls as his destination, how clearly have you erred! Your journey is not yet over, only the one who walks through the door reaches the city, "**So enter homes through their doors.**"[128] If you but raised the flag of understanding in the convoy of thoughts, how swiftly would you be supported by the banners of intimate knowledge (*ma'rifa*).

My Dear, fear of what Allah has written for them cuts the hearts of the righteous, until the worry of their hearts is moved by the remembrance of the Beloved. The soothing breeze of late-night prayers caresses them with the drafts of seeking forgiveness. They are responded to with His words, *"Is there any to ask of Me?"* If not for the coolness of their sweat of exertion, they would melt from the fire of worry. Their precious breaths, more fragrant than foreign incense.

My Dear, this sermon is medicine fit for bodies and souls. For the *arifeen,* it is a welcoming gathering. For the repentant, it is a gathering of mourning. For those who have attained completion, it is subtle indications to vast meanings. For those who are beginners, it is words to contemplate.

My Lord, You have unleashed my tongue in the arena

---

128 Quran 2:189

of expressions, with agreeable praise of You, and with pleasant descriptions of Your friends, who are the most beloved of creation to You. Their meadows boast to their listeners like spring does to winter.

My Lord, solidify the goodness of what You have bestowed upon us of Your *tawheed* till our dying breath. Make us among those, who on remembering the blaze of their sins, douse it with a deluge of tears. Have mercy on us by those whom You have accepted from amongst us. Those whom You have transmuted from the copper of sin to the purest gold. O Most Merciful of those that show mercy.

Part Fifteen

The praise belongs to Allah, who unlocked the locks on the hearts of the *arifeen*, enabling them to discern subtle realities. Who bolted the locks of wretchedness upon the hearts of the disbelievers, the blasphemers, and the wicked. He perplexed the minds of the knowing ones with their immersion in the ocean of His Greatness, and the pearl-diver returns with riches.

He unfolded the garment of the sky on the canvas of space, and bejewelled it with the gems of stars and planets, mesmerising minds through the mastery of His creation. He set the cosmic bodies into orbits and ornamented them with the Sun and the Moon. He inscribed therein constellations upon the backdrop of night, studded with the redness of Mars, the glass white of Jupiter, the splendour of Venus, and turquoise Mercury – making them all roam in tune with His decree.

The hand of His power masterfully ordered the dominion of His kingdom, and whatever else was to follow. He split mankind into three battalions for as long as they are led by the march of night and day. The first is in the loins of their fathers, destined for wombs. The second are the soldiers of the wombs, destined for this world. The third are those of this world, destined for decrepit graves. Eventually, all will be gathered to be divided into two. One in the bliss of Paradise, the other, imprisoned in Fire. Indeed, the soldiers of this world will be overcome, vanquished will be their homes, and the world to come will prevail. This is the outcome, as transcribed on the esteemed Tablet.

So Glorified be the One, Who measured all things by precise measure. The *arifeen* read the pages of existence and understand, with the minds of their inner sight (*baseerah*), what is hidden from sight. Their hearts roam to catch sight of lofty meanings, in secret and in open. Alas, what is it with these others, that they fall to the lowest pit?

I praise Him with the praise of a slave who entrusts his affairs to divine decree. I testify that there is no god except Allah, Alone, no partner has He – a testimony through which I hope to reach safety from the chastisement of the Fire. I testify that Muhammad is His slave and messenger, the chosen, selected Prophet. May the prayers and blessings of Allah be upon him, his family, his companions, and followers.

My brethren, what is with the heart of your resolve, that it quivers? What is with your heart's sight, that it is veiled? What is with your record of good deeds, that it has faded? What is with your following the path of guidance, that you have gone astray? What is that makes you desire this dark, shadowy world?

Woe to a scholar content with superficial terms instead of underlying meanings. Who clings to outer forms, emptying them of their essence. His mind fails to comprehend, and his heart's sight is blind. But if the guide sleeps who will lead the caravan? They have hoarded the goods of knowledge upon the scrolls of their hearts but have not ventured into the city of action. Were they to present their deeds to the judge of sincerity, their pretences would bow in humility. They would be bound in the prison of God-fear, fearing to speak even when asked to deduce legal opinions (*fatwa*).

The tree of action, rooted in knowledge, is like "**a good tree: its roots firm and its branches in the sky,**"[129] standing firm in a storm. But the tree of seeking fame is like a leaf failing to soar in the wind of "**Unto Him ascends the good word, and He uplifts the righteous deed.**"[130]

Is There Any Knowledge Without Action?

It has been related that one of the scholars who would perform many righteous deeds, more than he would seek extra knowledge, was asked about that and he replied:

I dreamt that it was the Day of Judgement, and a call was given out calling all the scholars. I made to move forward with them, but it was called out to me, *"O you! You have lost knowledge. May Allah make you lost!"*
I called out, *"But I was devoted to seeking knowledge and study!"*
He said, *"Woe to you! Is there any knowledge without action?"*
I awoke in a fearful state, and promised myself that I would remain persistent in action until I meet Him.

One of the pious predecessors said:
When it is the Day of Judgement, and people are driven to the place of gathering, a caller will cry out from beneath

129 Quran 14:24
130 Quran 35:10

the throne, *"O gathering of scholars, come forth."*

They will stand in rows until a woman will appear on a fast-moving mount of light. The scholars will see her and lower their heads. The caller will call out, *"O gathering of scholars! This is Rabia al-Adawiyya! She performed righteous deeds but did not study. What have you all done with what you have studied?"*

My Dear, watery eyes are chapters in the book of remorse. When they flow, their lessons are taught. Tears are the conclusions of their expressions.

How regrettable that when the caravan of the determined, untiring ones ventured in the depth of night, your ears were muffled by the blanket of being held back. The hearing of your heart was sealed with "**but Allah was averse to their being sent forth.**"[131] You consumed the alcohol of sins, so you succumbed to the drunkenness of sleep. Failure to meet the conditions chained you in the prison of slumber.

My Dear, those who taste the sweetness of closeness with the Beloved in the seclusion of night, gladly sell their sleep for awakening. How many nights have you squandered in impiety? Is it not time to retire in the valley of remorse, where the land is fertile and breeze fragrant?

O you, upon whom the winds stir up white hairs, as you drift towards the shores of old age, the ship of life

131 Quran 9:46

shipwrecked. Hasten! Cling to a piece of wood, float back to the sanctuary of repentance! Not all has sunk, salvage what remains, "**what is left by Allah is far better for you.**"[132]

Chilling cold strikes when the sun's light is veiled for an hour. What becomes of a man who veils himself from the enlightenment of his mind for fifty years! When the light of *tawheed* shines for the *arifeen*, they ascend upwards. When it darkens they stand in prayer, seeking divine support.

My Dear, the door of humility is nearest at hand. Enter your tale there amongst other, aspiring ones. When Adam, upon him be peace, turned the chapter of "**Our Nurturing Lord! We have wronged ourselves,**"[133] it was followed with the conclusion of "**so He accepted his repentance.**"[134]

My Brethren, we have gathered together, but no tear has been shed. We depart our separate ways, not humbled, nor shaken. I stand beside you, equally ashamed with the unfurling of my tongue about my own shortcomings.

By Allah, my Brethren, help me in weeping for even a moment to disperse the grief of our hearts. Perhaps the scent of the shirt of *Yusuf* shall come our way with the glad tiding of acceptance.

My Brethren, whomsoever of you delight with finding the

132 Quran 11:86
133 Quran 7:23
134 Quran 2:37

Beloved, let him mention that I acted as His ambassador. Ask Him to grant me too of what they have been granted.

My Lord, I have admonished Your slaves excessively. Here they are, each of them carries from this admonition whatever they can bear. All journey to Your door, hopeful of benefiting and attaining Your gifts. My Lord, do not return them empty-handed, disappointed, and refused. Grant them, and me, Your spiritual gifts. Make us to continually receive Your mercy, O Most Merciful of those that show mercy!

Part Sixteen

The praise belongs to Allah, Who meticulously records the deeds of His creations in ledgers since before time. No shrouded crime is hidden from Him. With the hand of balance, He measured out provisions, and He measured out life-spans sufficing those provisions.

He established the dome of the sky upon pillars of His power, studding it with stars in constant motion. He rotates the wheels of celestial bodies upon the pivotal axes of the North and South Poles. By His command, they embark, and then return. He bejewelled the sky's robe with two brilliant lights, one of which eclipses nearby stars. The other, with the intensity of its blaze, leaves no sign of any other. He made their setting points set out on the horse of the constellations, so that it might be known by their departure, that this, our finite home, is passing too.

He made this world like a rose of spring, a lifespan limited to dreamy tales and the poet's imagination. How many loved ones have withered away? How many friends have faded back into its soil? No remnant of them remains.

He is the Forbearingly Kind, who wove body and soul together in subtle ways that powerful minds are impotent to comprehend. He causes the eyes of clouds to shed tears of rain over the lifeless bodies of vegetation. In short time, you see they are revived, reaching upwards in yearning embrace. And all this is proof of the resurrection of decrepit skeletons.
By Allah, how excellent are the *arifeen,* who placed all

their hopes in the Beloved. Their aspirations are aimed towards the highest of the high, and their souls yearn the captivating presence of the Beloved. He honours them with the garment of not relying on creation, of paying heed to the melody of His signs, and with contentment with seclusion with the Beloved, and so they enjoy a pleasant life. He lifts the veil of heedlessness for them, and they contemplate Him clearly, with pure hearts.

Indeed, Glorified be He, Who already has vanquished His creation with the creation of death, subjecting all past ages to the sword of annihilation. I praise Him, with the praise of one anticipating His succour in removing the suffering of the scorching fire. I testify that there is no god but Allah, Alone, no partner has He – a testimony I prepare for when the agonies of death subside. I testify that Muhammad is His slave, and messenger, who, with his message, awakened sleeping souls and frivolous minds. The prayers and peace of Allah be upon him, his family, and companions – a prayer I hope will rescue from the horrors of the Day and the terror of the guards of Hell.

O seller of his life for a paltry price, you have squandered both the price and the goods. O prisoner in the jail of heedlessness, if only you peered into the valley of night, you would see palaces on the riverbank of "**Little of the night did they slumber.**"[135]

You would hear nightingales of their longing, yearning upon the branches of "**and before dawn, they seek forgiveness.**"[136] Happy are their moments of sleeplessness,

135 Quran 51:17
136 Quran 51:18

vigilant against slumber. They are in seclusion with their Beloved, conversing deep into the night with trembling hearts.

An Eloquent Madman

One of the righteous narrates:
I once noticed a boy laying on the ground, spreading himself over dirt, making a pillow with his right hand, and sighing loudly. I was with another, and I said to my companion, *"Let us see what the matter is with this sick one."* My companion said, *"He is not sick. This is one who appears to be inwardly sickened with love, and outwardly, but a little slave."*

I neared closer to him, and noticed he was a youth wearing a worn, tattered, woollen garment. I heard him say, *"What a wonder that one reaches knowledge of You, and tastes the sweetness of Your love, and is then removed from serving You."* He continued repeating this until he lost consciousness.
I said to my companion, *"By Allah, he is certainly struck with some malady of madness."*
He regained consciousness and saw us. He said, *"What is the matter that you look at me?"*
I said, *"Perhaps we can offer some medication for the illness from which you suffer."*
He replied, *"Truly, the One who tested me with the illness, He is the One who has the cure. However, it suits the sick one to treat himself by going on a diet."*
I asked, *"A diet of what?"*
"A diet of leaving what is forbidden (haram), turning away from sins, contemplation of the King, All-Knowing, voluntary

prayer at night (tahajjud) when the people are in slumber, consuming only what is sufficient for one's needs, patience at the time of trial – at times of discontent and joy, chastity and contentment at the time of wealth, preparation for death, studying to answer the questions of Munkar and Nakir[137]*, and getting ready for the standing before the King, the All-Powerful. Then, it is either to Paradise, or the scorching Fire."*

He wept tears upon his tears, inducing us to weep profusely too.

We said, *"We are your guests, please pray for us."*

He replied, *"I am not the horse of that arena."*

We persisted and pleaded till he said, *"May Allah make His forgiveness your banquet when you meet Him. May He make Paradise your destination. May He make the remembrance of death constant in my mind and yours."*

We continued on our way, our hearts being revived from the excellence and beauty of his words.

My Dear, this is but madness brought by love for the Beloved. O "sane one" what preaching can sway you? How do you measure up to them?

O one clinging to the rope of earthly desires until exhaustion. Woe to you, how have you seen it fitting to keep the company of *iblis*[138] and expel the angels? You have been deceived by fake gold ever since you had forsaken knowledge as your appraiser. If you see the mind preferring the cheap over the valuable, know the mind has warped. Had you realised so at the onset of

137 The two angels that will question one's faith in the grave.

138 Another name for shaytan or the devil.

lusts, you would have recognised its deformity.

Your life has not gained the necessary provisions, as your occupation is mere sleep. Only those with ample provisions can join the ranks of the generous. And only those ascending the Prophet's steps of emulation are crowned with acceptance.

How peculiar it is, I have pierced the canvas of your ears with many arrows of preaching, yet I have not hit the target. Surely, if darkness prevails before the bow, little hope does the archer have. "**Nor was it you who threw but it was Allah Who did so.**"[139] The preacher is, himself, but short of the aim.

The Hidden Shirk

One of the righteous narrates:
I spent part of my life in preaching and giving admonition, but I did not find my words having an effect on others nor my own heart. I became disturbed because of this.
One night I dreamt someone say to me, "*Be sincere, purify your words from the polytheism (shirk) of worldly ambitions, you shall find your words settle in hearts and minds.*"
I awoke, my sickness having been diagnosed.

My Lord, tether our ambitions to the hope of Your forgiveness. Make all our words sincere, seeking Your face alone.

---

139 Quran 8:17

My Brethren, a foretime, gatherings would be adorned with speeches from the likes of *Junaid al-Bagdadi, Marouf al-Karkhy*, and *Shibly*. They were such, that when they drunk the spiritual drinks from the cups of His love, would water all those present. Such are the gifts of the generous. Alas, what sorrow is the loss of such cherished guides and companions. They once were, and now they are no more.

O one whose heart's earth is barren. When will it blossom with roses of righteousness? When will your state change? When will the stains upon your heart be cleansed? When will you liberate the captive that is your faltering resolve? O one slaughtered with the sword of "I'll do it tomorrow!" O one whose concern is taking his full of his stomach and genitals. O people besieged by armies of spiritual misfortunes and griefs, this is but a funeral. A eulogy for our dead hearts.

The caravan of productive lives has left, here you are, trailing far behind. If you do not catch up soon, how easily will you be cut off from them. With determined resolve, seek His help! Be a refugee amongst the righteous, perhaps His compassion and pity will carry you forward.

Like a Child with its Mother

A man came to *al-Danouri* while he was preaching and said, *"O Shaykh, what can I do? Every time I come to one of the doors of Allah, I am turned away by trials, tests, and misfortunes. They cast me upon the earth of heedlessness!"* The Shaykh replied to him, *"My son, be at the door of your Master like the little boy with his mother. Even if she slaps him, he throws himself at her lap. Every time she pushes him away, he humbles himself before her. He stays like that until she sympathises with him and embraces him."*

Suppose He has averted you from His door. Which door could you set out for? Which path would you tread? Which direction could you face? Rather, persist with your knocking at His door. It may open for even the most unworthy guest!

Alas, how we yearn for the company of the masters of the heart. Alas, how we long for those nights of friendship with the Beloved. Alas, for those clear days brimming with obedience.

My Dear, if you cannot join the vanguard of the lovers of Allah, then beware lest you fall behind the ranks of the repentant ones, those earnestly seeking His forgiveness. Woe to you, how often will you bid farewell to the caravans of the repentant, only to return back? They have arrived while you have lost your way. They have reaped the profits of their aspirations, you face bankruptcy. If you fail to take revenue from the fruits of the season, what profits would you seek?

My Lord, illuminate our hearts with the light of Your forgiveness. My Lord, enrich our time with what pleases You. My Lord, bring order to our scattered minds and confused states with Your excellent mercy. My Lord, safeguard the one who surrenders to Your decree. My Lord, do not let trials overpower us – those that sever us from You, O Most Merciful of those that show mercy.

Part Seventeen

The praise is due to Allah, Who sowed the seeds of love in the fertile hearts of the *arifeen*. Each one's heart quivers with the bloom of its blossoms. He watered the gardens of their hearts' depths, stirring it to sincerity. The breezes of His kindness palpitate over its valleys, clearing it of dust and impurities. Thus, they excelled, one of His many marvels. They yearn for Him, and out of longing their tears flow.

He drew some close with the rope of felicity, while others, He distanced with wretchedness. The gazes of the *arifeen* and the fearful are awake late into the night. Each eye opposes its opponent of sleep. Their determination strides under moonlight to the heavens of intimate knowledge of Him (*ma'rifa*), for Allah's sake they ascend and descend those hills.

The gem of their souls, polished by the treasure of His guardianship, shine brightly, illuminating their path. With them as keys, He opened the locks of high, spiritual stations and subdued obstacles and barriers. Those chosen ones concealed their ranks deep in their contemplation, their homes abound with righteousness in private. Greetings and salutations to those engrossed in His love, their elevated stations revealed through the sincere testimony of their tears.

Glorified be He, the One Who answers the call of the distressed when they call upon Him. He is the Responder to prayers, the Hearer of them all. I praise Him with the praise of one who flees to Him from destructive sins. I testify that there is no god except Allah, Alone, no partner has He – a testimony like one who hears and obeys the command of his Master. I testify that Muhammad is His slave and messenger, who wielded the pickaxe of prophethood and shattered the stronghold of disbelief and its fortresses. The Quran is his witness, that he rescues sinners and acts as their intercessor. The prayers and blessings of Allah be upon him, his family, and companions as long as birds sing their myriad melodies.

O bearer of his sinful coffin upon his own shoulders! How terrible is what you carry. O raiser of the flag of evils, how terrible is what you have hoisted. How drunk have you become with the cups of "I'll start tomorrow" from the waitress of procrastination? How often do the guards of worldly pursuits prevent you from entering the sanctuary of His protection? You but gather prosperity for your grave, and you will answer for it. You suppose yourself victorious and triumphant. In reality, you are defeated and overthrown. Others enjoy your wealth while you agonise in your grave, and they won't tire in spending.

Your heart is absent from the congregation of prayer, lost in the marketplace. Where are you when you say "**I direct my face...**"?[140] Woe to you if the convoy of lusts settles permanently, but that of longing for Allah is a

---

140 A reference to one of the opening prayers during salat (prayer). The entire wording being - "I direct my face to the One who originated the heavens and earth, as one on the true, monotheistic religion. As one who surrenders to Him, and I am not one to ascribe partners to Him. Surely, my prayer, my sacrifice, my life, and my death are for Allah, Nurturing Lord of all worlds. No partner has He. Thus was I commanded, and I am but one of the Muslims." – Sahih Muslim, Book 6, Hadith 240.

temporary guest. When will you expel that permanent settler? When will you embrace that delightful guest?

Alas, where have they disappeared, those stars guiding the way, those suns of bright spiritual stations, those healers of those fallen on the path, those proofs for confused minds. They have departed, little trace remains. Their homes deserted, no news of them circulated, "**Here are their dwellings, uninhabited after them save for a few.**"[141]

O one whose heart roams in the valleys of heedlessness. If the land of righteous deeds is spoiled, from where could profits be reaped? *Khidr* showed patience with *Musa,* upon them be peace, with three disobediences, before *Khidr* said, "**This is the parting between you and I.**"[142] How many moments of disobedience have you accompanied?

My Brethren, beware of sins, for they have humiliated whoever is humiliated. Even the noble crown of "**Prostrate to Adam**"[143] fell to the earth when the head of "**O Adam, dwell you and your wife in Paradise**" had to bow, humbled after an act of opposition.

O travellers, where are your ready provisions? O wayfarers, where are your prepared mounts?

---

141 Quran 28:58
142 Quran 18:78
143 Quran 2:34

The Merchant's Insight

One of the righteous narrates:
We would travel to Mecca, may Allah keep it honoured, every year. One year, we found a man selling wheat and we bought some from him. He weighed the wheat for us, and we returned.

On the second year, he weighed the wheat for us again. But when we returned the third year, he said to us, *"Measure the wheat you would like to purchase yourselves."* We said, *"We have not known you to do this in past years?"* He replied, *"It appears that you do not travel every year, from (spiritual) station to station. What a shame! What a shame!"*[144] We were left speechless and amazed at his state.

But alas, you, stricken with (spiritual) poverty, have been persistent in accumulating sins for the past fifty years! Your vow of repentance shatters within a year's span. Where is the unwavering resolution of the determined ones? Where is the anguish of the remorseful?

O slumbering one in the wastelands of "putting things off till tomorrow." You have truly lost your way. The

---

144 It appears the wheat trader had, during the past three years, advanced in his piety and righteousness so much so that he was able to recognise that these men coming to him were honest and would not cheat him by weighing the wheat themselves. In one hadith (Tirmidhi 3127) it has been narrated that the Prophet, peace and blessings of Allah be upon him, said, "Beware the intuition of the believer. For verily, he sees with the light of Allah." Then, the Prophet recited the verse, "**Verily, in that are signs for those of discernment.**" (Quran 15:75).

child of your heedlessness says, *"When I get older, I will repent..."* But sins and obstacles on the path reply, "**Far-fetched, far-fetched is that which you are promised.**"[145] The sign of death on the sick one is their procrastination of treatment. The foundations of your hopes are "**on the brink of a crumbling bank.**"[146] Your determination for repentance begins like a soaring eagle, but at the moment of truth, you flee like a common crow. You break apart the integrity of your oath by delaying action. "**Be not like she who unravels her yarn, breaking it after it had been strong.**"[147] Would you rather, that every time your hair whitens, your book of deeds blackens? Will you have it that every time your strength weakens, your (spiritual) sickness strengthens? Every moment your life shortens, do your empty hopes increase?

The Reality of My State

Hassan al-Basri narrates:
One night I pondered my state and measured myself with the Quran. But I did not find myself either amongst the people of Paradise, nor the people of the Fire.

As for the description of those in Paradise, I measured myself with His, Most High's words, "**Truly the believers have prospered...**"[148] and did not find myself amongst them.

I looked to the description of the people of Hellfire in His, Most High's words, that they say, "**We were not**

145 Quran 23:36
146 Quran 9:109
147 Quran 16:92
148 Quran 23:1-9

among those who prayed, nor did we feed the poor, and we engaged in vain discourse with those who do the same, and we denied the Day of Judgment."[149] I found myself as one who prays and who believes in the Day of Judgement.

I remained confused at my state until I heard a voice shout out from a corner of the *Ka'ba*, "*Not from these, nor from those! But rather from '****And others who admit their sins; they mixed righteous deeds with others that are evil. It may be that Allah will forgive them.****'*[150]"

Thus, my affair was cleared up for me.

O you sick with sins, when shall you seize the salve of remedy? When the two contestants, sickness and health, appear before the judge, and the decision to eradicate the sickness is endorsed upon the parchment of disease, it is not long before the fever of worldly lusts flares up again. If one is not submerged in the first, he succumbs to the second affliction.

My Dear, if the wolf shows affection to the lion, then know it is but a ploy. When you see the lion of reason captivated by the wolf of worldly desires, know that it is a trap. So contemplate how to save yourself from that snare!

What a wonder it is, that so many advices by eloquent

149 Quran 74:43-46
150 Quran 9:102

tongues cry out, but fall on deaf ears. But rebuke does nothing for the one infatuated with himself, for the lover's eye sees no fault.

Know that musk is from the impure blood of an earthly gazelle. When it is separated, it is placed in the pouches of kings. Ambergris is the waste of whales that the sea excretes to its surface, where it gathers and solidifies, having no fragrance. But when it leaves its abode, it is precious and fragrant.

But you, O jewel of creation! Know the value of your worth! Woe to you, remove yourself from the darkness of your sinful nature. Venture into the realms of your mind to value the preciousness of your being. Indeed, it is beyond price. Was there any announcement more treasured in the marketplace of creation than "**that which I created with My two Hands?**"[151]

How strange that *iblis* wanted you removed from the home of the King and was banished because of you! Yet now you follow that outcasted wretch and abandon the King? And still He calls out to you as if saying, "*My slave, return. Let not this separation be lengthened, nor your alienation intensified.*"

Woe to you, if you cannot attain the humility of the *arifeen,* then do not forbid yourself the humbleness of the repentant. Perhaps divine sympathy will gaze upon you. My Lord, I have said everything I could and compiled it.

151 Quran 38:75. Reference to Adam, upon him be peace. Full verse being, "**O iblis! What has prevented you from prostrating unto that which I created with My two Hands? Did you (just) become proud? Or have you always been arrogant?**"

My Brethren, we sinners share a common predicament. We have begun to weep over our past shortcomings and tears have begun to flow from the springs of our eyes onto the channels of our cheeks.

My Lord, do not make our profit from this gathering be mere eloquent words and crocodile tears. Anchor our aspirations as You have anchored those of the ones who have reached You. Overfill our vessels with Your forgiveness, and grant us charity because of our poverty before You, O Most Merciful of those that show mercy.

End of *The Soul of Souls*

Other Titles by Dhikr.

The Illumination on Abandoning Self-Direction,
Al-Tanwir fi Isqat Al-Tadbir.
Ibn Ata'illah Al-Sakandari

Sayidah A'isha: Wife to the Prophet,
Mother to A Nation. A Short Biography.
Dr Muhammad Said Ramadan Al-Bouti

The Reviver of the Second Millenium:
Imam Al-Rabbani.
Shaykh Osman Nuri Topbas

dhikr.com.au

www.ingramcontent.com/pod-product-compliance
Lightning Source LLC
Chambersburg PA
CBHW061123100726
47911CB00013B/663

* 9 7 8 0 6 4 5 0 3 7 9 6 8 *